D   Jue

MAR

MA

MAY
JU

22.

JUN

The Team That Jack Built

THE TEAM
THAT
JACK BUILT

Paul Rowan

MAINSTREAM
PUBLISHING

To Mick

First published in Great Britain in 1994 by
MAINSTREAM PUBLISHING COMPANY (EDINBURGH) LTD
7 Albany Street
Edinburgh EH1 3UG

ISBN 1 85158 670 9

A catalogue record for this book is available from the British Library

Typeset in Bembo by Litho Link Ltd, Powys, Wales

Printed in Great Britain by Butler and Tanner Ltd, Frome

Contents

Acknowledgments

Marla, Kathleen and Fergus, Julie and Anna, Paul Desmond, Donal Cullen, Bob Hennessy, Bernard, Rory G, Mary H, Senan, Paul and Kate, Maurice Walsh, Zinze, Kitty Barlow, Sharon Anderson, Paddy Farrell, Damien Weldon, BBC World Service News, Eamon and Jack.

Introduction

A SORT OF HOMECOMING

FROM WHERE I WAS SITTING, on a stool in a bar on 59th Street, Orlando was beginning to sound better backwards. Odnalro. An Orlando veteran, his pint of Bud spilling down his shaking hand, was pouring forth on the horrors of the place. It was so hot down there, he said, that he had to drape himself in soaking towels for the duration of the Mexican match. Another Irish fan had frozen with fear in the top row of the top stand and had to be helped down by the emergency services. 'Whatever you do, don't put me back up there,' he had pleaded, and they gave him a seat in the disabled section. They said he was suffering from vertigo, but it might have had something to do with the heat as well. And Charlton seemed to have gone troppo down there. The heat wouldn't let up, nor would Jack let up talking about it. Water on the brain apparently.

The bar on 59th Street was supposed to be a place of celebration for Ireland's qualification for the last 16 of the World Cup, confirmed by the draw with Norway, but the clients were muted. Likewise, there was no chanting on the bus back from the Giants Stadium in New Jersey to Port Authority. As the fellow from Douglas in Cork said, every silver lining has its cloud. In this case it was the return to Orlando as the second place team which was causing people to fret over the next game, even as they were celebrating qualification. The trip to the States had held out promise of Boston, Chicago, perhaps even a roar across Route 66 to California. Sex, drugs, rock 'n' roll 'n' soccer. Instead, the team was being jerked back and forwards, north to south, from the Giants Stadium to the Citrus Bowl on a thousand-mile-long yo-yo. And the bad vibe about Orlando left a sinking feeling that the string was about to become tangled at the end of its run. Who can we blame? Jack? Packie? Not yet. No. Walt Disney, Orlando creator? Wasn't he a fascist as well?

It was all terribly unfair. But when another man with a shaking drink pointed out that we were going to Orlando because Ireland had *beaten* Italy, we were now looking at a horrible injustice. Ireland had finished the group with the same number of points as Italy, we had scored and conceded the same number of goals, but because we had beaten the Italians, the man explained, we finished ahead of them in the group in second place.

So the prize for beating Italy was a trip back to Orlando, huh? Was this what our heroes had sweated blood for? Was it for this that McGrath, father of three, had risked decapitation, throwing his face in front of a ball curling from the boot of Roberto Baggio which looked destined to end up playing around Packie Bonner's net. Ireland's performance in the 1-0 victory against Italy scaled new heights of heroism. Even some among the rugby contingent which joined 50,000-odd Irish supporters in the Giants Stadium shed tears. In Dublin, the wall of the pub down the road appeared to expand and contract like a bass drum as the *Olé* chant slammed against it from those packed inside.

But Charlton hadn't stopped telling us how bad the match

against Mexico in Orlando was going to be, and he was right. In 110-degree heat, Irwin, Staunton and McGrath looked like they were trying to play in the Everglades rather than at the Citrus Bowl Stadium. Not only could Staunton not play, he appeared to be actually melting. The *Olé* chant was claimed, or reclaimed, by the Mexicans – Luis Garcia with his two goals was their matador – and the Irish fans never got it back.

It was not as hot, but very hot nonetheless, in the Irish yuppy pub in London, Minogue's. A broker from the city watched the match as though staring at a trading screen at the end of Black Tuesday. You couldn't hear or sometimes even see the telly, or get to the bar for a drink. Couldn't Mr Minogue have followed FIFA's and Charlton's lead and allow his staff to hurl plastic containers of beer around the pub? Mexico 2, Republic of Ireland 1, Mr Minogue 0.

Ah, the Giants Stadium. After the Orlando game, the names of some of the Norwegian team had a comforting softness. Ireland played delightful patterns through midfield in the first half as the Norwegians stood back, the poverty of ambition displayed by Norway making the Irish play seem almost Brazilian. In the second half, Norway gave some inkling that they were the side that had kept England from the World Cup, but the massed ranks of Irish supporters behind Bonner's goal collectively blew the ball off course whenever they threatened. Ireland were the team that finished stronger. One felt immediately afterwards that Ireland deserved to win for the amount of possession they had, but it was disappointing to reflect that they hadn't forced Thorstvedt to make a save in the match.

Which brings us back to the bar on 59th Street. Most of the fans weren't going back to Orlando. They were going home, or staying home in New York. Was that why they had chanted 'We Want Jack' at the end of the Norway game as though the World Cup campaign was over? It was like arriving at a party to find that the stereo wasn't working properly and half the guests, thinking better of it, were taking the last bus home.

Down in Orlando, even the cheapest motel had a big swimming-pool. The lady in the gas station beside it wouldn't sell alcohol after two a.m., recommending root beer instead. She didn't look a day over 35, had ten children, and she was working nights in the gas station to raise some extra money as her new boyfriend was encouraging her to go to college. She certainly wasn't doing it on a diet of root beer. A description of her as one of America's silent heroes brought a lovely warm smile, but she still wouldn't open the refrigerator containing the stacks of perspiring beer bottles. Morning broke on the day of the match with the sight of the root beer on the bedside table, a distressing start to the day.

Right, brace yourself, a trip into the tropical molasses. Or was it possible to actually jump straight from the balcony about six feet across, into the swimming pool? A thought surfaces. The air conditioning is not on, so why am I not standing in an oven? A tentative step outside confirms that there might not be the chance to sweat a gallon for Jack's Army. It's hot, but overcast; not as bad as New York. The sense of foreboding dissipates. There's no reason why Ireland can't compete in this. And Ireland's record against Holland is an improving one. Defeat in the European Championships, a draw in the last World Cup and victory in a recent friendly in Holland. The party is still on for the true believers. Dallas and the next round come into view. Wouldn't it be great to rent a car with a few other lads and drive through the Deep South? How was it that Paul Simon described the Mississippi Delta on *Graceland*?

By midday, kick-off time, it was still comfortable. The massed ranks of Dutch and Irish supporters seemed to mirror the equality between the two sides. No thoughts that by half-time Ireland would be torn apart, back-pedalling in midfield and run ragged down the flanks. Two goals from two mistakes alright. But the Overmars' sprint down the wing and Bergkamp's strike after Phelan's misplaced header had an authority and composure that was lacking in the Irish. Then there was Bonner's goal. Jonk had strolled past Sheridan before unleashing the shot which Packie contrived to scoop into his own net. I'm sure lots of people thought of it, but somebody in the next row couldn't resist saying, 'I told you so'. It's widely described as a schoolboy error, but this gives schoolboys a right to feel the way animals must feel when they are compared to football hooligans. More another nail in the coffin of the Scottish goalkeeping clan. In the second half the Dutch stood back and the Irish, to use Jack's phrase, ran their bollocks off – but life's not like that at this level.

A ghetto, a black ghetto, lies between the Citrus Bowl Stadium and the centre of town – apparently every American city has one of these. Folk sit around the street, cadging cigarettes or selling water. I'm sorry Ireland didn't win, man, one says, they deserved to. Damn right you can feel sorry for me. My hopes were raised, and then dashed. I've come to the United States for two football games, two very important football games, and haven't even had the satisfaction of seeing Ireland score a goal. And the Dallas Odyssey is off.

Grieving back in my hotel room at the way Ireland had been outmanoeuvred and the general unfairness of it all, I was shaken by my room-mate, Jerome McAteer from Co Down. He's already told me that he's Jason McAteer's cousin, and if the Irish had beaten the Dutch he was going to become his brother. Snap out of it, he said, there's still a party to enjoy. I conjure with the thought of never going to, or watching, a football match again. I take it too seriously, get too wound up and then don't wind down. I am a bad Irish fan. But it's somewhat reassuring to hear that there is the debate going on back in Dublin too. Do we party, again, reflect more solemnly on the performance of the team and the course it should now follow, or turn our minds, for the first time in three weeks, to something different altogether?

Before, there would have been no question. Another vital Ray Houghton goal, the one scored in the victory against England in the European Championships in 1988, was enough to provoke a big party, even though Ireland didn't win another match in that competition. The Government, city authorities and the FAI are in no doubt this time around either. They started organising a homecoming party after the victory over Italy. Forward planning is required to prevent the mayhem which surrounded the team's return from Italia '90. They hadn't told the players or Charlton about this party because they felt it was an unnecessary distraction. But the stage is already half-built in the Phoenix Park where the Pope said Mass and half a million people are expected.

However, this time the players don't want to go back to Dublin for a party. They had been so disappointed by their performance against Holland that they had left the stadium without speaking to the press – except to those newspapers who had paid money into the players' pool to receive their thoughts. Jack isn't so disappointed, but he's adamant he's not going home because he has got one of his jobs to do with ITV in Dallas.

At one stage the party back in Dublin is cancelled; workers leave the stage half-completed. Then the Government orders it back on again. The players have changed their minds, they've cancelled their holidays, most of them are coming home. But Charlton is displaying one of his most endearing features, railing against the consensus that he should return.

Jack has to face his first wave of public discontent with his conduct as manager. He is intensely irritated to hear that an RTE chat show has interviewed a man who thought the team was waiting to be paid to come back. Charlton has always said that the main purpose of Ireland's involvement in the World Cup is that the Irish can have a good party – and now that they're having one he isn't showing up. John Giles, writing in the *Evening Herald*, shows the common touch that was noticeable by its absence when he was Ireland's first big manager, in the seventies. Jack Charlton should return home, he writes, 'out of respect for the people who supported him and the team in an unbelievable way through the World Cup and the qualifying campaign. Many people spent a great deal of money to follow the team in the States, some who could not afford it, and Jack should acknowledge that by returning.'

From the moment Charlton took the manager's job, the FAI have lived in fear of him walking out. He has threatened to do so on several occasions over issues that would appear trivial to other managers. The homecoming fiasco, as it has now become, has all the ingredients for a classic Charlton stomp. Public discontent, arm-twisting of the players and himself by politicians and bureaucrats, his commitment to the team and the fans called into question. Instead, Charlton, bombarded by phone calls in the middle of the night at his hotel in Orlando, relents, like a parent appeasing an insistent child. He will fly home for the celebrations and return to Dallas by Concorde.

With the main guests there under sufferance, it was clearly not going to be a party at all. In the end, it was the Irish people who didn't show up. It was Thursday morning, a working day. About 30,000 arrived in the Park for the festivities. Many were teenage girls screaming at Jason McAteer, Phil Babb and Gary Kelly, the threesome who had acquired pop star status during the World Cup.

When the party petered out, the debate about the team's future took over in some earnest. Replacements would have to be blooded, or discovered, for a huge chunk of the team which had been its mainstay for years – Aldridge, McGrath, Cascarino, Houghton, Whelan, Bonner and Moran. The triumvirate of McAteer, Kelly and Babb would only fill some of the gaps.

For the first time there was also a debate about the future of the manager himself – was he the right person to take on the challenge of forging a new side? Eamon Dunphy, in the *Sunday Independent*, his most outspoken critic, called for his resignation – 'Charlton is only a small town hero', he wrote. Peter Ball in the *Sunday Tribune* questioned whether Charlton should resign. A straw poll in the *Sunday Tribune* found that ten per cent – a startlingly high figure – thought he should.

His tactics were disputed – should he have used a 4-5-1 system, had he played the right formation? But the most serious question hung over how he had fared in psychologically preparing his team, in particular over the trip back to Orlando. Charlton won a victory for all teams when he persuaded FIFA to allow players to take water during games. But his constant complaints about the heat and his ongoing battles with FIFA created a phobia about Orlando in the Irish camp which the players had to fight to overcome. When Ireland took the field against Holland, when the conditions were at their kindest, the team appeared to be in a Mexico mindset. In both games they were two-nil down before they made a serious effort to take control of the game. Some said that Charlton, unlike his players, seemed to harbour no serious ambition to reach the later stages of the competition.

Charlton is right when he says the Irish team, and its fans, have helped put the country on the international map. I visited a pub in Stuttgart with a friend in 1980. We asked for a beer, and the proprietor asked where we were from. When we told him, he pulled an imaginary submachine-gun from under the counter and began pumping us with imaginary bullets. Now his images of Ireland would be drawn from the exemplary conduct of the thousands of Irish fans who visited the city during the European Championships in 1988.

The level of disappointment over USA '94 is also a measure of how much Charlton has achieved. But, as is clear from the aftermath of USA '94, it's no longer enough for Ireland simply to get there, and to be there. Charlton is a man for an emergency, a heroic figure. Searching for a historical comparison, I stumbled dangerously out of the world of sport, to Churchill, who led Britain through the Second World War, but was not seen as the man who could win the peace.

Charlton was an aberration, who came from nowhere to find that the Irish players and fans were disillusioned, while the football structures were corrupt and crumbling. It wasn't a war, it was only a sporting crisis, but with Charlton at the helm and a nation longing to have something to celebrate more than victories in the Eurovision Song Contest, the journey out of it would have its epic proportions.

Chapter 1

JOURNEYMEN

POLAND. ALWAYS POLAND. Ireland were always playing Poland. 'I got 43 caps for Ireland, probably about 40 of them against Poland,' says Ray Treacy, a provider for Ireland up front in the sixties and seventies. 'Myself and Tomaszewski were like blood brothers, and most of the players knew each other by their first names. We'd kick in down the same end before the match.'

In fact, only nine of Treacy's caps were against Poland, most of them away from home. The Football Association of Ireland was well treated over there, the officials were well looked after by the Poles. Dollars could be changed for the local currency, zloty, at up to ten times their face value on the black market. It was always a great place to buy cut-glass for virtually nothing once the money was changed. The trips spawned a number of business deals. One council member of the time used to buy ladies underwear in bulk from Poland for sale back in Ireland.

Discussions on the exploits of former Irish soccer teams inevitably lead back to Poland. The FAI secretary, Joe Wickham, died of a heart attack at the match in Katowice in 1968, while Ireland were being beaten 1–0. Joe Kinnear, the Wimbledon manager and the former Tottenham Hotspur player, has Poland to thank for some of his most vivid experiences of playing for Ireland. In 1970 the Irish party was travelling from Poznan in western Poland by train, the eventual destination being West Berlin for a game against West Germany. A few miles outside Poznan, the train stopped, it shuttled backwards and forward and the carriage in which the players were seated was taken away. 'All the directors had seats and we were left in the luggage compartment sitting on cases. We had to sit on top of the luggage for miles. It was a hell of a journey. It was amazing because the next day we were due to play West Germany in their last match before the World Cup. The least important people there were the players. There was no thought that these people needed to be looked after. Most of the officials came for the beano, for the laugh and the jolly up.'

The football did have its place, somewhere. 'I'm not sure there were more officials than players, but there were more officials than were needed,' says Treacy. 'In many cases there would be a large number of officials when we arrived in Warsaw, yet on the evening of the game, in Katowice, or Wroclaw, or Krakow, a lot of those officials hadn't quite made the game. They had stayed in Warsaw, in as nice a hotel as you could find over there. Things were good and they were having a good time. That was normal.' Normality would get worse before it got much better.

Chapter Two

VINTAGE

WHILE THE POLES looked after the FAI, the Irish were particularly generous to Spain. But there were rewards for helping them qualify for major championships. Ireland, Spain and Syria had been drawn together in the qualifying group for the 1966 World Cup in England, but Syria, incensed by the treatment of African countries by FIFA, had pulled out. The tie between Ireland and Spain was played over two legs – Ireland beat Spain 1–0 at Dalymount Park, but were hammered 4–1 in the return match in Seville. Goal difference, then, counted for nought. With the dust hardly settled on the Seville tie, the FAI General Secretary, Joe Wickham, went into lengthy negotiations with the Spanish FA on the venue for the replay, rather than leave it to the discretion of FIFA. At one point there was an adjournment; Spain, it was reported, wanted the Irish team to remain in the country for the replay, or fix the game for Portugal, the Irish were holding out for London or Manchester. At around three a.m. the two sides emerged with a compromise – the replay was fixed for Paris.

Forty thousand people turned up for the replay, nearly all of them from the Spanish community in Paris, then swelled by Franco dissidents. A single Irish Tricolour was spotted amid a sea of red and gold flags. Ireland hung on till ten minutes from the end when a goal from Ufarte put the Spanish through.

The circumstances surrounding the match illustrated the depth of suspicion that existed between some of the players and their masters in the FAI. In the run-up to the game there were reports in both French and Spanish newspapers that the FAI had accepted a sweetener from the Spanish FA during the negotiations that Joe Wickham was involved with in Seville. The papers said that the Irish had agreed to the Paris venue in return for receiving Spain's share of the gate receipts and all the fees from television rights. The total gate receipts amounted to some £25,000, three times the annual income of the cash-strapped FAI. The Spanish FA denied any wrongdoing, but the reports of a secret deal also spread around Dublin. Arthur Cunningham, then a director of Shamrock Rovers who had close contacts with the FAI, told the Irish goalkeeper Pat Dunne.

The Manchester United and Irish full back, Tony Dunne, was one person who took exception. 'I had become a winner then, I wanted to win, so you can imagine my disgust when I learned that the Irish officials had agreed to play the game in Paris in return for the gate receipts. It had to be the biggest disappointment of my career because it was certainly the biggest opportunity to qualify in my time, and with the finals in England, who knows what might have happened?'

'We were aware of it, but we accepted what was going on,' says Dunne's Manchester United team-mate and the Irish captain that day, Noel Cantwell. 'We didn't have any player power or anything in those days.'

The other unusual thing about the Paris game was the presence in the Irish team of nearly all its star players such as Dunne. In 13 years representing Ireland, Dunne only won 33 caps, though he was picked, according to one estimate, about one hundred times. 'You will find that although I was picked for a lot of games, I only played in about half of them. Often I had injuries, but on other occasions, Manchester United, through Matt Busby, influenced me not to play, and saw to it that I didn't lose out on the match fee, in order to safeguard me from getting injured. I was willing to accept the situation because the man, as far as I was concerned, could do no wrong. He was the one who used to say, "you're injured, you're not going", and I would already have my ticket for the plane.'

Dunne remembers one time in particular, at Arsenal, when himself, and his United and Ireland team-mates Cantwell and Shay Brennan were about to travel to Dublin and Busby stopped Dunne as he was leaving the dressing-room. 'Where are you going?' Busby asked.

'I'm going to play in Dublin.'

'You're not, the other two are gone. You're injured, you've gone over on your ankle.'

'I haven't gone over on me ankle.'

'You're injured.'

And that was it. End of story.

'It's been known at Old Trafford particularly and at Arsenal that sometimes people would just fake injuries,' says Cantwell. 'Matt might say to somebody, "I don't want you to go." Okay, if they pay your salary, they give you the few quid, then you say, right, you've got a little knock, a pulled muscle, and you didn't go.'

While the little knocks were a problem for the Irish team, the main difficulty was that the international set-up, such as it existed, had little to do with success on the field. Home matches were played on a Sunday afternoon at Dalymount Park. The ground didn't have floodlights, so the only other time to play the games would have been during a weekday afternoon, but then the attendances would drop sharply. The Sunday arrangement meant that Don Revie, Bill Nicholson or Matt Busby weren't going to let their players go over when they might have a midweek game in Europe.

For the players who turned up the most arduous part was often the journey itself. Charlie Hurley, the Irish captain and centre half for much of the sixties, had to come from Sunderland. 'You'd finish at five o'clock on the Saturday, and then get a police escort to the station, and then to the airport. It was sometimes impossible to get a plane, so you'd have to take the boat.' For the boat, the next stop was Liverpool, for the overnight sailing to Dublin, a journey of ten hours.

'I came over on the ferry for the game against Spain in 1965. It was the most frightening experience I ever had in my life. It was full of queers and everything. You'd pin your arse to the bunk. You'd get to Ireland in a terrible state on the Sunday morning. Then there would just be time for a hot bath to loosen up. I would say that over the 40 caps, if anyone ever earned them it was me.

'I wasn't one of the guys who ducked out of the big, hard games. There were an awful lot of times I used to turn up on a Sunday after playing on a Saturday and Giles, Tony Dunne, Cantwell, a lot of these people, got knocks, and couldn't play. I never did that.

'Right through my 40 caps we could have given some tremendous games to a lot of teams. But, oh, the amount of times we turned up with six players missing and you'd see two or three guys coming from League of Ireland football, didn't know anything about international football, absolutely in awe of it all.'

It was in these circumstances that Ireland again obliged the Spanish. Ireland were bottom of the group in the qualifying round for the 1968 European Championship, the Nations Cup, propping up Czechoslovakia, Spain and Turkey. Czechoslovakia had beaten the Irish 2-0 in Dublin, and only needed a draw at home to qualify for the finals ahead of Spain. Ireland went to Prague in desperate straits. Giles, Cantwell, Dunne and Brennan were missing from the team. On their previous visits to Prague, Ireland had been beaten 7-1. As the team bus made its way to the stadium, the crowd gestured to them that the score would be

10-0 rather than 7-1. 'We started off playing 4-4-2 and we defended continuously for 45 minutes,' says Hurley who was also the coach at the time. 'About ten minutes into the second half John Dempsey scored an own goal. They didn't need that anyway, they were giving us a real pasting. I changed the system to 4-2-4; it took a bit of guts because being beaten one-nil out there wouldn't have been a terrible result for us. But we scored two goals in the last 20 minutes and won 2-1.'

Spain were amazed and relieved at qualifying. 'Ireland's victory,' said the President of the Spanish soccer federation, Jose Luis Costa, 'shows the professional honesty of its players since they had already lost their hopes of qualifying for the quarter-finals before this game.' The Spanish FA sent over two crates of wine as a token of their appreciation. The FAI council agreed 'that in respect of the present from Spain, a bottle of wine be given to each player who travelled to Czechoslovakia, and the balance left be partaken at the last council meeting'.

Charlie is still waiting for his bottle.

Chapter Three

THE FALL OF THE BIG FIVE

EAMON DUNPHY, sports journalist and social commentator, is perhaps the most hated man in Ireland. To Philip Greene, the veteran Irish football commentator, he is, 'a little so and so'. Eoin Hand, the Irish manager before Jack Charlton, poured a glass of wine over Dunphy at Joy's nightclub in Baggot Street, Dublin. Later on, Dunphy's comments on RTE during the World Cup in 1990 that he felt shame at the way the Irish team had performed enraged nearly the whole nation. In pubs in Dublin his subsequent appearances on television were greeted with chants of 'Eamon Dunphy is a wanker, is a wanker' – and the chant also resounded around Lansdowne Road. Jack Charlton holds much the same opinion, which he spits out rather than chants.

But it was Dunphy who was at the centre of a mini-revolt by the players which changed the face of Irish international football. As a York City player, Dunphy made his debut for Ireland in the Spain game in Paris in 1965. Like many Irish players from the lower divisions of the English League – he later settled at Millwall – Dunphy rarely missed the opportunity to get away and play for his country. It was something of an adventure to escape from club football and there was a special camaraderie amongst the players. Otherwise, he says, 'it was a bit of a joke playing for Ireland. The honour of playing for your country if you're a professional footballer or indeed in any sport is directly related to the honour that's inherent in the organisation.'

With the death of Joe Wickham, a widely-respected figure, during the game against Poland, that relationship deteriorated even further. 'We were told in the dressing-room after the match,' says Dunphy. 'After a couple of minutes silence, someone broke the ice by enquiring if he had signed our cheques, or The Message, as it was then called. That's how footballers are.' Because it was behind the then Iron Curtain, the body had to stay there for three or four days while the red tape was sorted out. 'An appalling row broke out among the accompanying officials as to which two of them would have the honour of spending a further four days in Poland. It was an appalling, sordid business,' says Dunphy.

'On another trip to Poland we saw a senior FAI official propositioning a young prostitute in the lobby downstairs. Myself, John Giles and Joe Kinnear went to our room and we phoned his room and we bartered with her. We found out that he had offered her a bottle of duty-free Scotch and two hundred duty-free cigarettes which was an absolute fortune at the time, so we decided we would liberate her from that by offering her whatever it was, with no services required. And she left his room to come to our room and the little fat fucker followed her naked down the corridor looking for his Scotch and duty-free cigarettes back.'

Giles was the Irish team's best practical joker as well as its outstanding player – and his perceived attitude problem was to lead to a major flashpoint. When he was dropped from the squad for a World Cup qualifying game against Denmark in

Copenhagen in 1969, it seemed his ability to enrage and embarrass officials during the long boring hours on away trips counted for more than his skill on the field. His place in the squad was taken by the Shelbourne player, Billy Newman. Don Revie's reaction to Giles being dropped was one of mock enthusiasm: 'If this guy Newman is better than Giles, I must sign him for Leeds immediately.'

The team to play Denmark was picked, as was the norm, by the 'Big Five' – a committee made up of representatives from a cross-section of Irish football, from junior level to the League of Ireland, who were elected on a yearly basis. The Big Five had long been resented by players, especially those based in England, where Alf Ramsey had moulded a side that had won the 1966 World Cup. The committee would pick the team and then hand over the reins to a coach just before the match. As player-coach at the time, Charlie Hurley was the man responsible for handling the Big Five's teams. 'You'd get some real potato pickers coming to play,' he says. 'A selector with a bit of clout would want to pick one of his own boys. You have a League of Ireland player capped and right away he's worth a few thousand quid. An awful lot of that went on.'

Giles' omission from the game against Denmark was the catalyst for change. He had snubbed the selectors when recalled to the squad for the following fixture, a World Cup qualifying game at home to Hungary, getting Leeds to tell the FAI that he was unavailable for selection. In effect, Giles was on an undeclared strike from international duties. As the day of the match approached, Giles came to Ireland all right, but to play at a golf competition at the Hermitage. Ireland lost the game 2-1, Giles won the golf competition. Giles did return to the squad for the next game and found the players were united in anger at the way he had been treated by the FAI. They had a meeting at their hotel and formed their own committee to organise some form of protest. The committee – Giles, the goalkeeper Alan Kelly (whose son Alan is now in the squad), Tony Dunne and Dunphy – then met in Manchester.

They were a curious group of conspirators. For Dunphy, a member of the Labour Party in Britain since 1963 and a prominent member of the Professional Footballers Association, the agitation had to be seen in a wider context. 'This was after the Prague Spring, this was after Czechoslovakia in 1968, a time of reform, we thought.' For Giles, who had only four important things in his life – family, football, golf and sleep – it was a little simpler than that. 'You had five selectors who just weren't qualified to pick the team. You can't have five people picking the team. They had no experience of playing for or managing a side. It was just stupid.'

At this stage Mick Meagan, who had won 17 caps in the midfield for Ireland, had replaced Charlie Hurley as player-coach. The players' committee – with Dunphy drafting the statement – called for Meagen to be appointed manager and have the sole right to select his own team, a system that had been introduced in most other European countries since the early sixties. In October 1969, before Ireland's match against Czechoslovakia, Giles and another squad member, the Shamrock Rovers player, Frank O'Neill, presented their demand to the International Selection Committee. 'The FAI knew in their hearts that what they were doing wasn't right, that other countries were passing them by,' says Giles. But Giles was aware that the officials had a lot to lose by catching up: 'We told them that they could keep their selection committee, they could still have their trips. But that the manager would have sole right of selection.'

To accommodate this fudge, the officials were able to reach a compromise with Meagan. He would attend meetings of the selection committee at which the team panel would be picked. Meagan would then have the right to pick the final eleven. It was the first nod of recognition by the FAI to the way the modern game was developing.

Shortly afterwards, the FAI capitulated to a second demand, this time led by international players from the domestic league in Ireland. They threatened to boycott the

European Championship game against Sweden unless the FAI recognised the Professional Footballers Association of Ireland and granted it a seat on the FAI council.

There were further changes – introduced this time not through coercion but through co-operation between the FAI and the new manager. Home games were switched from Sunday to midweek. Now, instead of rushing straight from the airport or the ferry, the players, at least those released by their clubs, could gather the day before the match for training. For the first time, the Irish players could be seen jogging round the Belfield campus at University College, Dublin. Belfield was just a stroll across from the Montrose Hotel in the comfortable setting of south Dublin suburbia, which had replaced the low-budget Four Courts Hotel in the centre of town as the team's headquarters.

These were encouraging signs, but something was desperately needed. The year 1971 was a landmark for Irish football, marking the 50th anniversary of the breakaway by the FAI from the Irish Football Association in Belfast at a time of bitter sectarian division. The anniversary was more an occasion for sober reflection rather than celebration. The Republic of Ireland hadn't won a game in nearly four years and were becoming one of the laggards of European football. To mark the anniversary, the FAI had organised a game in May at the end of the season with the English FA, which was being touted as a full international. But Irish officials had been horrified to learn that the FA was planning to send over a second-string team, brought together for a forthcoming promotional tour of Australia and that no caps would be awarded.

The FAI ruling body is the Council and, by the time the English match was due to be played, there was a disgruntled air among its members as they gathered for their monthly meeting. Four days before, Ireland had been beaten at Lansdowne Road by Italy, the 17th successive home game without a win. Some members were prepared to lay the blame for the continued run of bad results at the feet of manager Meagan. What's more, the

English FA had announced a panel consisting of second and third division players for the Golden Jubilee celebration – it was clear the event was going to be a huge anti-climax.

At the start of business a member of the selection committee, Patsy McGowan, announced that he was resigning, saying that he had to travel 300 miles from Donegal for committee meetings where he no longer had any role. Having aired his personal grievances, McGowan then broke ranks with an outburst against the organisation: 'We started out in national football 50 long years ago. But I would say that without doubt we have not made the slightest progress in that time, on or off the field.

'We have, I believe, 28 members of Council and, let's face it, what the hell are we doing for the game at this level? You are there to represent your clubs and it ends at that. As far as I am concerned we are a burden on the FAI purse strings. We all look for our trips to the countries we play in, and if we don't get them, we have the neck to go to the next meeting of the Council and have a go at the selection committee and the manager about taking an extra player and how much that cost.'

He ended his remarks with a salvo across the Irish Sea. 'I don't want to close without expressing my disgust at the English FA for refusing to bring a full international side to Dublin for our Golden Jubilee match. All I can say is "Damn poor show, sir". This is where we should have made a stand and told them to stuff their third-rate side and look elsewhere.'

McGowan's fiery defection didn't stop some Council members expressing their suspicion and resentment of the arrangement between Meagan and the selection committee. Their comments were to spark off the worst confrontation so far between the players and the FAI. 'Who picks the team?' one council member, Ray Prole asked, reflecting a widely held belief that Meagan was an ineffectual manager influenced unduly by senior players. He said 'the old pals act' applied to team selection and said there were some very good players at Cork Hibernians who were not selected. A former selector said, 'I don't agree with Mr Meagan's appointment as manager and I'm sick of all the favourable comments I read about the manager.' A member of the selection committee, John Farrell, joined the attack on the manager. 'Unfit players have been played,' he said. 'When I asked Mr Meagan if Eamonn Rogers was fit on Monday night [when Ireland played Italy] the manager replied, "He is ninety-nine per cent fit".'

These comments were reported in the Dublin newspapers the next day. Meagan regarded them as an unacceptable public display of dissatisfaction with his management, and he announced his resignation.

It was a dangerous time for Irish football. Seamus Devlin in the *Irish Times* pointed out at the time: 'The little men obviously want their share of the limelight, even if it does mean reverting to the outdated system of selection by the self-selected "Big Five" and a possible breach in relations between players and headquarters.'

The 'little men' had, however, chosen a bad time to organise such a counter-revolution. The international squad was in the middle of a three-week spell in Dublin during which they were playing three matches – against Italy, the England Eleven, as it was now called, and Austria – and the news of Meagan's resignation provoked deep unease amongst the players. They fulfilled the Golden Jubilee fixture, grafting a 1-1 draw with an obscure England selection consisting of Grummit, Hindley, Stephenson, Wall, Mills, Eddy, Piper, Keen, Chilton, Wagstaff and Bridges. Two days after this fixture, three of the players – Dunphy, Dunne and Kelly – met four officers of the association of Merrion Square with a mandate to threaten strike action for the following game against Austria if they were not favourably received. As it happened the FAI officials – led by the President, Sam Prole, who was sympathetic to the players – promised to use their influence with the Council to satisfy the players' demands.

The battle between the players and the more conservative elements on the Council was again swinging in the players' favour. What they now needed was to keep the pressure on the Council. They decided to seek directly the support of the public which had long become suspicious about the commitment and motivation of their national team. The players called a press conference at the Montrose – Dunphy, Dunne and Kelly were again the main spokesmen. They told the press that they had been given assurances by the FAI that there would be no return to the selection committee method and that the selection committee may be done away with altogether. Dunphy then answered the allegation that Meagan's team selection was 'an old pals act'. 'Every player accepts his decisions,' Dunphy says. 'If Alan Kelly, Steve Heighway, Johnny Giles or Tony Dunne were dropped, they would merely fight harder to get back on the team.'

The question of the commitment of the Irish players was raised. The players pointed out that the clubs frequently refused them permission to travel, and they urged the FAI to contact Sir Alf Ramsey and find out the dates of England's matches, so that Ireland's could be played on the same day – a measure that would be introduced many years later. Alan Kelly said: 'If we had no interest, as the knockers accuse us of, if we did not want Ireland to go places, then why should we have bothered asking for a manager, asking for the FAI to meet us this week and now inviting you gentlemen to talk to us and help us?'

The players then issued a written public statement which was clearly marked with the Dunphy stamp: 'In view of the recent controversy surrounding the international team, we would like to express our feelings clearly to the public. We feel that over the past year since the appointment of the team manager there has been a great improvement in our approach to international football.

'We have failed to achieve results which in the long term is the best way – indeed the only way – to pass judgement on the system. But in international football a year is a short time, particularly in view of the difficulties of getting players released for international duty.

'Yet in a year there have been radical changes in our preparation for international games. Proper and lengthy training sessions, long overdue, and attempts to develop young players for the future by including them in the squad. But above all the belief, sincerely held by all the players, is that at last we have a future in this class of football.

'For the first time all the players want to play and are proud to be part of an exciting challenge. Our aim is not for one great result. We want consistent results. To play with our heads as our hearts. We are in the development stage. We have played only a handful of games [under Meagan]. When Sir Alf Ramsey took control of England, with all the talent at his disposal, they were knocked out of the Nations Cup by France. It took time even with England's resources. Northern Ireland likewise took a number of games to get results. They have had their crises. We are having ours now.

'In appointing a team manager the FAI showed great courage and vision. They have critics within their own ranks but have indicated that the present system will continue. We are sure that the vast majority of the public support Mick Meagan. We feel this is true also of the members of the Council.

'Despite the knockers we feel we have a future in international football. Therefore we would urge Mick Meagan to continue the job he set out to do. His dedication has been an inspiration to all of us.

'This is not an easy time, not least for the public. We appreciate that. But success is not easily gained. We would like you to help us meet the challenge by giving us your support. Given that, we will not fail.'

They were ringing words, which raised the stakes for the Nations Cup match against Austria the following day. However, the Austrians appeared not to have read the script. They achieved their biggest ever away victory, beating Ireland 4-1 at Dalymount Park. Dunphy had a nightmare game and was substituted at half-time at his own request, claiming mental exhaustion. He ended his weeks of agitation on a humble note.

'I feel that our international future now lies with the young fellows. All I want to do is slip quietly back to Millwall and just play for my club.' He would never play for Ireland again, but he certainly wasn't slipping away quietly.

★

'Pathetic, pedestrian, puerile,' fumed Peter Byrne in the *Irish Times* after the match. 'If we must find out the price of international success the hard way far better to do it with a team built around home-based players.' It was a familiar cry which was put to the test in the return leg of the Nations Cup away to Austria. Ireland, decimated by injuries and withdrawals from the English-based players, fielded ten League of Ireland players and were beaten 6-0. In between the two Austrian games, Mick Meagan had been sacked and the FAI had also turned to the League of Ireland for its new manager, Liam Tuohy. For Tuohy, it was a start of a long involvement with Irish international sides that was to end in a bitter fall-out with Jack Charlton.

Tuohy had let his interest in the Irish job be known for some time. At the height of the players' conspiracy against the FAI, he had approached Dunphy in the Montrose Hotel and offered his services for the manager's job, but was given short shrift. Tuohy had useful credentials: he was a former Irish international; he had been appointed player-coach at Shamrock Rovers in 1964 and they went on to win the FAI cup five years in a row; he had also been manager of League of Ireland selections. When approached for the full international job, Tuohy was manager of Dundalk. 'When I applied for the job I had an interview and I just outlined what I would like. I told the FAI that I wanted sole team selection. I was unhappy with the idea that somebody was going to pick 16 players and say to me, "There you go. Make something out of that."'

As it happened, the FAI, at its annual general meeting, had already agreed to scrap the selection committee after the hiatus of the previous two years. Tuohy took on the job on a part-time basis in September 1971 for a salary of IR£500 a year plus the match fee of IR£50.

Tuohy was an unknown quantity amongst most of the English-based Irish players. His immediate priority was to try to earn their confidence and respect. The 6-0 drubbing in Austria had made it perfectly clear to him that a team drawn from the League of Ireland could not cope at international level. Tuohy went to England to speak to a number of club managers. 'I wanted to meet them face-to-face rather than being an unrecognisable voice at the end of the phone asking for the release of players.'

Tuohy's first stop was Leeds, where he wanted to meet Don Revie. Since being dropped by the selectors two years previously, John Giles – besides his early involvement with the players' committee – had virtually disappeared from the Irish international scene. Leeds had heavy commitments in Europe and the club had made it clear to the FAI that Giles was unavailable. It was a tricky early test of Tuohy's management skills. 'The word was that Don Revie was very annoyed with the FAI over the way John was treated,' says Tuohy. 'I flew over to Leeds unannounced because I felt that if I announced I was coming over Don wouldn't see me. I arrived at the training ground and I saw John first. John said, "Okay, leave it with me." Then I met Don Revie. I explained that we were now trying to approach it in a more professional manner. And that John would be looked after, not just in preparation for the match, but that there would be a doctor available. A lot of clubs were concerned that fellas were going back with injuries which weren't being treated.' Tuohy was able to come to an arrangement with Giles and Revie: 'I was aware of the demands on Leeds being a top team. I did say I wouldn't ask John to play in any Mickey Mouse friendly matches, but for the World Cup qualifying matches I would. So I brought Giles back into the fold. But I couldn't have done it without going over there.'

The FAI had arranged for Ireland to play in a two-week summer tournament in Brazil involving a number of lower order international sides. It was known as the Mini World Cup but it was clearly in the Mickey Mouse category. Giles wasn't going, but Tuohy tried to obtain the services of Ireland's budding star, the winger, Steve Heighway.

Heighway was an enigmatic figure. He was born in Ireland of English parents, but only spent the early years of his childhood there. He was regarded, in footballing parlance, as an English lad, but it wasn't this which set him apart. Rather it was his degree in Russian studies and his quiet withdrawn demeanour. His Irish roots were discovered by a journalist when he was still in the Liverpool reserves, and the other Irish players were intrigued by this aloof college boy when he joined the squad. He roomed with Shay Brennan in the Four Courts Hotel, and when Brennan was asked by the players to give a character reference for Heighway, he replied, 'Well, he doesn't piss in the sink like the rest of us.' Rather, Heighway used the one available bathroom at the end of the corridor.

Heighway's club form, however, compelled Tuohy to try to make him an established part of the Irish set-up, and he went to see Bill Shankly to try to secure his release for the Brazilian tour. 'Shankly told me that he wouldn't object to him going but that Steve Heighway had told him that he was tired. But he gave me permission to speak to Steve. Steve said that he did like playing for Eire, but that he needed the rest. I couldn't get Tony Dunne from Manchester because he was going to get his tonsils out or something like that. Jack Charlton can get a premier division team out and have five or six premier division players sitting on the bench. The most I had were four first division [as it was then called] players and often the reason they were available to you was because they weren't in the first team.'

The reticence of certain top players made it clear that Tuohy had a credibility problem, but the players who made the trip to Brazil were pleasantly surprised with their new manager. The team achieved some good results, beating Iran — Ireland's first victory in 20 games — and Ecuador, while losing narrowly to Chile and Portugal. The manager showed good tactical awareness and was an excellent motivator. Tuohy was also a clever politician. He was aware of the players' antipathy towards the FAI, and he exploited that to create a bond with his squad. As players and a collection of FAI officials relaxed together under the Brazilian sun, Tuohy exclaimed: 'I have the perfect relationship with the FAI. They love me and I fucking hate them.'

'I couldn't believe I was hearing this,' says Ray Treacy, one of the players on the trip. 'The officials sort of looked at each other and sniggered. They treated it as a joke. We all knew it wasn't a joke. Up till then Liam was a guy we didn't really know, but this made an impact on the players. He certainly now had our attention.'

Whatever about his feelings towards the organisation, Tuohy was in fact working quite well with the FAI. 'Everybody criticises the Football Association, but they went along with what I asked for, even though they hardly made any money from it.'

The trip to Brazil had been organised in preparation for the qualifying rounds for the 1974 World Cup. It was now becoming standard practice for the team to gather on the Sunday night for the game on the Wednesday. Ireland beat France 2-1 in a World Cup qualifying match in 1972, the first home win in six years, then lost at home to the Soviet Union. They prepared for their away matches with a slim chance of qualifying.

Problems still remained when it came to the availability of players, particularly Heighway. Heighway had dispensed with the etiquette of putting his absence from the squad down to a groin strain or 'a knock' – instead he had again told Tuohy that he was just too tired to play. Tuohy was equally blunt: 'I deplore the player's attitude in connection with what must be regarded as the Republic of Ireland's most important encounter for many years,' he said. 'It is the best chance we have had to qualify in the past decade and if he is tired, then Giles must be a hospital case.'

Tuohy's *own* workload was a genuine health risk. He was holding down three jobs at the time. On the football side, he was managing Shamrock Rovers as well as the Irish team. On one occasion he had gone to spy on France in Paris. The match was on the Saturday night and Tuohy flew back into Dublin on the Sunday. He then drove straight down to Athlone for a Shamrock Rovers match against Athlone Town and arrived at half-time. On Monday morning Tuohy had to report for his proper job, as a sales manager for HB ice-cream. He also had a growing young family to support. His sixth child, a boy, Liam Jnr, was born while Tuohy was with the Irish squad for a friendly game, away to Poland. On hearing the news, the players presented Tuohy with an enormous Polish pram – 'the size of a small car' – which he wheeled through airports on his way back to Dublin. It was a touching end to Tuohy's spell as manager.

The trip to Poland was sandwiched in between Ireland's World Cup away games in Moscow and Paris. A 1-0 defeat in Moscow ended the chance of qualifying, and Tuohy was faced with a choice. He sacrificed the Ireland manager's job, the most tenuous of the three he held. 'At that stage it wasn't the big deal it is now to be manager of Ireland,' Tuohy says. 'We only played three or four matches a year so it was a fairly low-key appointment. I was sorry to leave it, but I just didn't have the time to do it. I had to make a decision as to which job to leave. Rovers was my week-to-week situation, while on the international side there was nothing coming up for a couple of years. And I really couldn't see us going anywhere.'

Chapter 4

A FOOTBALL MAN

ON A SPRING DAY in 1965, in a League match between Leeds and Manchester United at Elland Road, John Giles and his midfield opponent John Fitzpatrick moved in to contest a bouncing ball on the half-way line. Giles got there first, but went over the ball and slammed his studs into Fitzpatrick's right knee.

It was a destructive tackle mastered at Leeds by Giles, to which Don Revie would turn a blind eye. As Giles later confessed: 'To do it properly you have to have nerve, timing and above average skill. You pretend to play the ball in tackling situations but instead leave your boot in so the opponent connects with your boot.' Fitzpatrick was stretchered off the field and straight to hospital. His cartilage were severely torn and, at 24, his footballing career was over.

'It was a very hard game then,' Giles says. 'I had had a few injuries myself and I was prepared to look after myself.' As a young player at Manchester United, Giles had his leg broken and ankle ligaments torn when scissors-tackled by the Birmingham City player, Johnny Watts. He was out of the game for five months and it was touch and go whether he would ever play again. 'John Fitzpatrick wasn't a shrinking violet. I would regret that he was badly injured in the knee. I didn't intend to badly injure him and finish him in the game. But you know it can be a consequence of what you do. So I was very, very sorry for John Fitzpatrick, but in the battle at the time I didn't stop to ask questions.'

This appetite for destructiveness cast a shadow over the great Leeds team of the sixties and early seventies, which had Giles at its fulcrum, a player renowned primarily for sublime passing skills and intuitive reading of the game. In an era devoid for the most part of television action replays, he was skilful enough, unlike some of his Leeds team-mates, to be able to hide the more sinister side of his game from referees and fans, though not from his fellow professionals.

That same ruthless, uncompromising streak was also in evidence in his dealings with the Irish international side. From the time of his first cap against Sweden in 1959, Giles realised that things weren't the way they should be. The team had a strip similar to the Irish rugby outfit, and Giles, standing at five feet five inches, was given shorts that came down over his knees. He was back in his home town, back at Dalymount Park where he had seen countless games with his father, a stone's throw away from where his parents lived on the Navan Road. But for Giles, this wasn't quaint, it was wrong. 'It wasn't professionally good to play for the Irish team,' Giles says. 'It did annoy me. And when you went into the big competitions there was no sense among the players that we were ever going to qualify. Players know, they can pick it up very quickly that something is right or not right. It was back to the old Irish thing, always champions at moral victories. As a nation, we didn't expect to win, the players didn't expect to win. If we won the occasional match that was good, but there was no real drive or feeling that we were going to do anything.'

From the professional set-up at Leeds, Giles was coming down a league when he did turn out for his country, but he never let his own standards slip. In the replay in Paris against Spain for a place in the 1966 World Cup, the players had gathered together two days before the game and most went straight out on the town. Giles was sleeping back in the hotel. As Giles' career developed, so did his disenchantment with the static Irish set-up, and by the early seventies, he was a regular absentee. His presence, however, still loomed large on the international scene. As Ireland's premier player in the English league he was regarded, by others though not by himself, as something of an ambassador for Irish football. And his international colleagues, when Giles was around, respected how he rationalised the game and had simple, logical answers to Ireland's problems both on and off the field.

Tuohy, having persuaded Giles to come back into the international fold, found he had acquired a valuable ally. 'To me, John was the ultimate pro. Every opportunity he would get, he would sleep, particularly before matches his preparation had to be right. He was a great example to the young people in the squad. He wasn't just there as a player, he would help out at the training. When he was there he wanted to do well, he wanted the team to do well.'

It was inevitable that when Tuohy's resignation came into effect in June 1973 Giles would be seen as the man to take over. He had the support of younger members of the FAI Council, such as Des Casey, Fran Fields and Louis Kilcoyne, who would all go on to be presidents of the organisation. The players agreed virtually unanimously that Giles was the best man – and several spoke to him urging him to take the job. Kilcoyne was deputed to telephone Giles and offered him the position.

'I wasn't that pushed about it,' says Giles. 'I was only 32 at the time and I was still playing for Leeds. But then I thought I might as well do it myself rather than somebody else come in and do it who's not going to do it the way I think it should be done.'

Giles, with the support of Revie, took the job on a part-time basis. But Giles was no ice-cream salesman; the FAI, albeit on a match-by-match basis, had secured the services of one of the most formidable young figures in the English game, immediately raising the expectations of fans and players alike.

Giles' first managerial test was a home game – a friendly against Poland. Four days earlier, the Poles had ended England's chances of qualifying for the 1974 World Cup by holding them to a 1-1 draw at Wembley. Against Ireland, they lost 1-0. Although only a friendly, it was a dramatic occasion – only the second home win in six years, and against the team that had effectively beaten the English. The problem was sustaining this type of momentum. The top teams weren't interested in playing Ireland, and friendly games against international sides of a similar standard ran the threat of incurring heavy financial losses which the FAI couldn't sustain. After Poland, Ireland wouldn't have another game for seven months, and it would be more than a year before they would play at home again.

The FAI, however, had been building up good contacts with the Brazilian FA – where they found Joao Havelange well disposed to them – and this led to a tour of South America in May 1974. It was to become an unfortunate coincidence for the FAI that from now on these exciting and ambitious trips to the southern hemisphere were to be affected by periods of intense political upheaval there. The team fared reasonably well on Ireland's first trip away with Giles as manager, but it was Dunphy, recalled to the squad by Giles after being banished by Tuohy, who snatched the limelight with his off-the-field activities.

On the itinerary was a trip to Chile, where six months previously General Pinochet had overthrown the Marxist government of President Allende and there was talk of thousands of people being murdered on the streets of Santiago. Dunphy, who had been active in the campaign against the Irish rugby team going on a tour of South Africa, was contacted by anti-Pinochet activists and asked to help organise a sporting boycott of Chile. 'What was being proposed was that we be the first international sports team to visit Chile since the coup and would therefore be used within Chile to show that the country was respected and respectable. Although I didn't feel that there was a case for a boycott, I didn't also agree with saying "There's nothing here that we have to think about",' explains Dunphy.

As the players gathered for a pre-tour training session at a sports centre in Crystal Palace, Dunphy was handed a number of leaflets by protestors which he agreed to distribute among the players. As he did so, one of the players ripped up the leaflets and told Dunphy that this had nothing to do with football. Dunphy's stand baffled and outraged the other players. 'Dunphy didn't have to go on the trip,' Ray Treacy says, 'but he nearly knocked a nun over in his rush to get on the plane.'

The team played Brazil and Uruguay, losing both matches narrowly. Dunphy was the victim of a practical joke. 'They gave me Mandrax, the heavy sleeping tablet. The Leeds players used to take them. They have been taken off the market now. You used to take a Mandy an hour before you went to bed. You'd get a high and then ten hours' heavy sleep. Giles was a master at it. They gave me two, and we were training the following day at five o'clock and I still couldn't walk straight.'

In the Chilean capital, Santiago, a midnight curfew imposed since the coup was still in place when the team arrived. The squad was staying at the Sheraton and Dunphy and Joe Kinnear were sharing a room. 'Eamon was reading those strange books as I called them,' Kinnear says. 'He seemed to get into some very intellectual books. He enjoyed them no doubt. Trotsky and whoever else it was.' About ten minutes after curfew, Kinnear and Dunphy heard shots outside their hotel window. They looked out and saw the body of a man being dragged out of a car by soldiers.

The game against Chile was played at the Nacional Stadium, where thousands of trades unionists, political activists and suspected opponents of Pinochet had been interned and murdered in the previous six months. When the players arrived at the stadium they noticed the walls of the dressing-room had been freshly whitewashed and some spotted bullet holes. Ireland won the game 2-1, their first victory over a home team in seven years. With Dunphy, who wasn't picked for the games, still feeling the effects of the Mandrax, all the players were able to return home on a high note.

The players had been happy with their first important experience with Giles as manager. He trained them hard, encouraging them to play attacking football and not to be intimidated by the reputations of such distinguished footballing nations as Uruguay and Brazil. At night time the players noticed that Giles would go to bed early and expect them to maintain their own self-discipline.

The full back Paddy Mulligan was one of Giles' biggest acolytes. 'John's ideas on the game and the standard he strives for are very high,' Mulligan said at the time. 'He's a man of total honesty, there's not an ounce of cynicism in his body. He gives players responsibility on the field and off. Lads are so used to being in England and being told what to do and what not to do, they find it refreshing to come back to him and be treated as adults, to be respected. And they respond. You won't find anyone in his team slipping out the night before the game, as you will in some squads. There are no cliques in the team, there's a very healthy atmosphere, it's all about caring. You don't feel you're on a conveyor belt and are going to be told to get lost tomorrow.'

Back home, Giles was seeking to build on the team's improved performances and maintain some continuity in the long spells between games. Giles organised some friendly games for his squad with English League teams such as Manchester United. For the first time, the squad gathered together for several days away from an international fixture. The venues chosen were, logically, English ones – the FA training ground which had just opened up at Bisham Abbey in north London and the Crystal Palace sports centre. The squad would do some light training and watch videos of forthcoming opposition in the

Nations Cup. Giles was working on both the tactics for the team and the players' frame of mind when they faced the opposition.

'What I tried to bring to the Irish team was sophistication and values that I had seen work at a very successful Leeds side, and eventually Liverpool. It was going back to the very basics of football. When you have the ball, be as constructive as you can and, when you haven't, do your best to get it back. In other words, just don't kick it for the sake of kicking it. Try and pass it. I would rather go square and back than go forward and give the ball away.

'But what I tried to instil into the players more than anything else was an expectancy to win. We're not going to win every match but if you deserve to win it, you win it. I wanted to get rid of the moral victory syndrome. I'd played in the Irish team over the years where you would go in afterwards and you'd say, "They weren't so good after all, we could have done them." I'd never agreed with that. I thought we had the players; we could go out and do it with a good positive mental attitude.'

By the time Ireland went into their first competitive game against the Soviet Union in the European Championship the following month, the squad had been better prepared than ever before. The Soviet Union were one of the best teams in Europe, but they were run off Dalymount Park by the Irish, with Don Givens getting a hat-trick. Liam Brady of Arsenal made a thrilling debut in midfield.

Expectations had never been higher. For the next game at home in the European Championship qualifier, a crowd of 50,000 turned up at Lansdowne Road to see Ireland beat Switzerland 2-1. But Ireland's away form let them down, losing by the odd goal in Berne and in Kiev against a Soviet team made up entirely of players from Dynamo Kiev who had won the European Cup Winners Cup final four days earlier.

Giles, however, was upbeat in his report at the end of the campaign to the FAI: 'In each of the qualifying groups the football world knew that there was one "easy" team. I knew that it would be anticipated that we were the "easy" team in our group. Events have proved to the contrary and at least we now have the satisfaction of having well beaten the group leaders [*the Soviet Union*]. This outstanding achievement in Irish football history has gained Ireland the respect of all football playing countries, for we are no longer the Cinderellas of Europe . . . I have every confidence that the present system, if it is permitted to continue, will in the future produce even better results despite the natural lack of resources of a small country.'

Irish football appeared to be heading on the right path, but Giles' own career was at a crossroads. Don Revie had resigned as manager of Leeds to take on the England job, and his great side was breaking up. Revie had recommended that Giles take over as Leeds manager; Giles, though aware that he would probably have to resign as Ireland manager, was interested but withdrew his name when it became obvious that the Leeds directors couldn't come to a unanimous decision. When Brian Clough took charge at Leeds, he left for another club. At the age of 34 he had become player-manager of West Bromwich Albion and Ireland.

While the wheels turned slowly at international level, Giles was an instant success with his club, which he had taken over after Don Howe was fired. Playing open, attacking football, West Brom gained promotion to the First Division in 1976. With his management pedigree quickly established, observers were linking Giles with the top clubs in the country. Instead, Giles was already planning to step off the management treadmill. Suddenly Giles announced, without giving a reason, that he was resigning at the end of the following season. Later he was to explain: 'Under the system that existed in England I could have done the "Double" ten years on the bounce and on the eleventh they could take on two directors who did not like the look of my face and I would be out. I could see no real end to management. I looked around and saw men like Jock Stein, Bill Nicholson, Bill Shankly and Tony Waddington, all managers in the classical sense who had done great things for their clubs and now they were out of business. They had been successful and they had been vulnerable. In industry, after comparable success, they would have been financially secure for life.'

It was clear that Giles wanted to get out of English football but his customary reticence about his next move led to a spate of speculation. 'A plush holiday-home in Ireland and membership of the local golf club point the way to Johnny Giles' future,' the *News of the World* ventured. 'He wants to restrict his soccer activities to managing the Republic of Ireland team and spending the rest of his time on the golf course.' The other good bets were that Giles was joining the exodus to the rich pastures of the Middle East or the United States.

The reality was closer to home – almost a year later, in 1977, it was announced that Giles would be returning to Ireland to become manager of Shamrock Rovers. He would also have an option to acquire 50 per cent of the club. It was a huge step for Giles and an enormous development for the domestic soccer scene in Ireland. 'Johnny Giles' taking over of Shamrock Rovers will provide Irish football with its greatest boost of the last decade,' wrote Bill Kelly in the *Sunday Press*, 'and at the same time it will provide Johnny with the biggest challenge of his soccer life.'

Where Giles had succeeded as a player at Leeds and a manager at West Brom, he was unable to meet the challenge at Rovers – and his return to Ireland would ultimately lead to him leaving the Irish international job.

Giles was coming to a domestic league scene which was in the doldrums – and Rovers' fall had been the heaviest of all. The glamour team of the League of Ireland, in the sixties Rovers used to attract crowds of around 10,000 regularly; when Giles took over they had fallen to around 500. A section of dilapidated terracing had been knocked down to make room for a car park. There was no longer any good reason to go to a football game, at Rovers or Bohemians or anywhere else. Before there was nothing else to do on a Sunday afternoon. Homes were more comfortable now. *Match of the Day* – where the best Irish players could be seen in the English leagues – and edited highlights made the game in Ireland look ordinary. Rather than cycle to the game, far better to go for a drive in the new car with the family. Or stay at home with the newly installed central heating on watching the telly, rather than stand on an open terrace with the rain pouring down and urine flowing past you from where the terrace wall had become a makeshift toilet. And for those who still wanted the excitement and glamour of the live sporting occasion, Croke Park was the place to be, as Dublin challenged Kerry's ascendancy in the biggest domestic sport of them all, Gaelic football.

Giles' belief was that to bring the crowds back to domestic soccer, excellence would first have to be achieved. His stated aim was that Rovers would be capable of winning the European Cup within seven years. His allies were the Kilcoyne brothers who owned and ran Shamrock Rovers – Barton, Paddy and Louis, his brother-in-law by marriage to Pauline Giles. The Kilcoynes, who had acquired new money through the family's successful construction business, owned Rovers since 1972, but had waited five years before they were ready to pump money into it.

Giles made Rovers the first full-time set up in the League of Ireland. He appointed two qualified player-coaches, Dunphy and Ray Treacy, who came with him from West Brom, and was joined by several other senior professionals such as Bobby Tambling and Paddy Mulligan. For a League of Ireland side, it led to a heavy wage bill, but the most ambitious part of the Giles plan was the creation of an apprenticeship scheme at Rovers. Most of Ireland's best players, Giles included, were snapped up by English clubs in their teens before they even made it to League of Ireland level. It had always been impossible for the Irish clubs to compete, but Giles felt he could now entice them to stay. 'Look at Brady, Stapleton, O'Leary, all from Dublin, worth hundreds of thousands of pounds and they hardly cost Arsenal a penny,' he said at the time. 'I've been 21 years in England. I'll be able to offer kids as good an apprenticeship as they'd get over the water. What's more, they'll be able to live at home. With the same coaching and the same facilities here, why should they go to England?'

Giles was back on the Dublin scene with a big job on his hands, but there was a section of the reception party which questioned his motives. For a person widely regarded at the time as Ireland's greatest ever player and most successful manager, Giles had a bad relationship with the public. His frequent, often unexplained, absences from the Irish side in his early days as a player meant there was already a pool of resentment and suspicion over Giles' approach to the international side. John O'Shea, at the time a soccer writer with the *Irish Press*, says, 'I felt that Johnny Giles didn't give a shit when he was playing for Ireland. Unlike people like Charlie Hurley and Noel Cantwell who would actually die for the country, Johnny Giles at a moment's notice would drop out of a match with a very suspicious groin injury. The bulk of the matches he played for Ireland he didn't appear to put it in.'

At Dalymount Park, as Ireland would be slumping to another heavy defeat, cries such as 'Fuck off back to Leeds' were commonplace. It was a response that dismayed his fellow professionals, who fêted Giles, and managers who were aware of the pressure the players were under. 'It wasn't unusual to hear remarks like "They're only over here for the money,"' says Liam Tuohy. 'It was more against the English-based players. If an English-based player didn't play well, he was only over here for the money. John Giles was often accused of it by fans. If he didn't play well, he didn't care, once he was doing all right for Leeds. This was the usual chant.'

There was a need for Giles to win over the press and public to get backing for what he was trying to achieve with Rovers and Ireland, but, while he was happy to talk about football, he made no effort to counter the bad feeling towards him and was generally perceived to be a withdrawn and even contemptuous figure. 'John Giles was the kindest man to a friend, but John didn't have many friends,' says Ray Treacy. 'He was the worst PR guy I've ever met in my life. He was the narkiest little whore. Somebody would walk up to him, it would happen ten times a day: "You remember me, don't you?" John would just say, "No, I don't remember you," out straight. He just didn't want to know.'

Giles' next major public announcement, typically badly mishandled, was to cast doubt on whether he had genuine commitment to his two jobs in Ireland. Four months into the Rovers job and shortly before Ireland were due to start their campaign for qualification for the European Championship, Giles announced that he would be spending the summer playing soccer in America, with the Philadelphia Furies. 'I believe,' he said, 'that this can be a very valuable exercise. We have a lot to learn from the Americans about football promotion and development.'

It wasn't a satisfactory explanation for Giles' critics who saw this as another example of him putting personal financial gain before the fulfilment of his main duties. Con Houlihan, the most celebrated sports columnist in the country, and a man not easily shifted out of his gentle disposition, ripped into Giles in the *Evening Press*: 'So now you know,' he wrote. 'The return of Johnny Giles was not altogether motivated by a starry-eyed ambition to make Shamrock Rovers and Irish soccer great again. Do you remember all the fine words that ushered in the second coming? Giles, like St Patrick when he was in Gaul, had heard voices and was coming home to convert the Irish . . . Are we to believe that his stint in America will not interfere with his work as Irish manager? Giles, needless to say, in announcing his plans to go west did not imply that anything as vulgar as money was involved – what he is doing is seemingly good for Irish football.'

Houlihan's comments struck a chord. In 1976 Louis Kilcoyne had helped organise an Irish testimonial for Giles, the first time such a benefit match had been held in Ireland for an international player or manager. Don Revie, then England manager, agreed to bring over a 'Don Revie Eleven' to play a 'John Giles Eleven'. Forty-five thousand people turned up at

Lansdowne Road to see a top-class line-up, but they were served abysmal fare. Incredibly for a testimonial, the game finished a nil-all draw with hardly a shot on target. Giles left the field ten minutes from the end. People whispered at the time that it was to count the money. The bad feeling increased when Giles, having announced that the testimonial game would be his last for Ireland, returned to the international scene afterwards and picked himself a further 15 times.

'There was resentment towards me that I was taking advantage of my position as Irish manager,' says Giles. 'There wasn't a feeling at the time of goodwill that this was a testimonial for 18 years' or 20 years' service, good luck to him. The feeling was "Ah, smart Alec, a match there." Liam Brady, Frank Stapleton and Dave O'Leary have all had testimonials in more recent times with goodwill. And I'll tell you one thing, I needed a testimonial match a lot more than they needed a testimonial match.'

The Irish manager, despite the public perception, was not a wealthy man. In one of his early forays into the business world, Giles had invested money in a company called United Insurance Brokers which had been set up in England by another Dublin man. The company offered a pension fund specially for professional footballers reaching the end of their careers. The idea was sound. Players involved in transfer deals were given an option; take the signing-on fee, officially five per cent of the deal, and pay the top tax rate on it; or leave it where it was, contribute some of your wages to it, and eventually you get it back at a later date. The business was a successful one, until funds were misappropriated and it went bankrupt in 1971. Giles, though under no legal obligation, had paid the players back with his own money. As a result, after ten years playing at the top level, he had lost all his money.

Playing soccer in America was a good earner – £40,000 for the summer in 1978. His decision to go to Philadelphia was announced to the media before he had informed the FAI. It also came at a time when he was involved in negotiations for a new four-year contract as Irish manager and it emerged he was looking for a substantial pay increase – from IR£6,000 to IR£9,000. The FAI made an effort to keep Giles from going, but then backed down.

Giles returned from Philadelphia four days before Ireland's next match, a European Championship game against Northern Ireland. It was the first time that the two Irelands had played against each other – and the game was seen not just as an important competitive game but as an opportunity to promote harmony between people on both sides of the border. The fans were on their best behaviour, but when the line-up of the teams was announced over the public address system, Giles' name was greeted with boos from a sizeable portion of the crowd. The mutterings had now turned to open hostility.

Ireland's style of play under Giles, involving a slow build-up with a premium placed on maintaining possession of the ball, where the ball was often passed back more than forward, was alien to a large section of the Irish crowds and deeply frustrating when the team wasn't winning. The match against Northern Ireland ended in a tortuously slow nil–all draw, and Houlihan resumed his attacks in the *Evening Press* in the form of an open letter to Giles:

'The job of being supremo of the Republic's team should be for somebody who is absolutely free from all other business, in football or otherwise. And since you are so involved with Shamrock Rovers and have financial commitments for good measure, you are not the man qualified for the job. Are you able to do the groundwork to your satisfaction? Have you seen any cross-channel games this season? Perhaps you went to Anfield to see how Gerry Daly is performing – or perhaps you stayed at home.'

Giles, at the age of 38, again announced his retirement as an international player before a home game against West Germany, but he was still heckled and jeered by a section of the crowd. A few games later Giles – on 16 April – resigned as manager as well. At a joint press conference with FAI officials on 15 April 1980, Giles ended his tenure on a typically reserved note: 'Since first accepting the position in 1973, the responsibilities of managing Irish teams at different levels have grown enormously and the job evolved to the point where it was no longer possible to combine it with my duties at Shamrock Rovers. As a family man, it meant that I was not able to spend as much time at home as I would have liked and that, basically, is the reason for my decision to resign.'

★

At his home in Birmingham, slumped in an armchair, 16 years later, Giles is prepared to expand on his explanation.

'If you go into reasons at the time, people think you're whinging. I wouldn't be into that. I said I wanted to spend more time with my family which was true. Once you're national team manager, you're public property whether you like it or not. People go to matches, they own a part of you, right? There was a lot of criticism, a lot of hostility, and my attitude was, I don't need this, I was doing my best for the Irish team and I'm not getting the reaction. That's people. It was hurtful for my family more than it was for me.

'I didn't think the booing was fair. The team weren't losing, I wasn't playing badly. It was just an image thing. I didn't handle things very well. I was a bit of a smart arse, I was a bit of a bread head. I was this, I was that. But people didn't know me. How could 50,000 people know me?

'I think I came across to the Irish public as a bit of a cold fish. I was never a character, never a real Dublin character. I think a lot of people didn't know what way to take me. I wanted things done right. I wanted things done professionally.

'I had a few disputes when I came in; people thought I was in it for money. I was never a money man. When I took over I did it for the same fee as I got as a player. When we got bigger crowds and moved to Lansdowne, well, there was a few quid in the kitty. And also, in those days, not so much now, if you're manager of the national side you belong to the people so the attitude is "Well, you should be glad to do this for nothing," and' – Giles raises his head from the armchair and laughs – 'sure, I was doing it for virtually nothing anyway. But when there was no money I didn't want any money and when there was money, I felt I should have been paid for it. I earned very little money, and had the reputation of being a money man. Jack is earning huge money and he has a name, somehow or other, of doing it for nothing. And good luck to him.

'People also thought that I was picking myself, giving myself caps,' Giles says, raising himself again from the chair and laughing again with incredulity. 'There was a feeling that I was actually giving myself caps, you know. I was 35, 36, 37 years of age, playing for the Irish team. It would have been easy for me to cop out but I wouldn't have been true to myself had I done that because I did genuinely think I could make a contribution. I played for the enjoyment and the glory of it. And when I started managing the Irish side it was ambition. I wanted to get rid of the inferiority complex from the days when we didn't qualify and we weren't expected to qualify. In many ways it brought a lot of criticism on me because the expectations became very high, very quickly, and after a year or two they were saying, "Gilesy, you've never qualified for a major championship", when we'd never been used to qualifying for a major championship before. But what was good about it was that people expected us to qualify. I wanted us, as a country, players and everybody, to expect to qualify. We were representing the country, and I thought it would be great, to make the breakthrough, to qualify.

'If I had my time all over again, I would definitely be more image-conscious. I didn't care about image. I was as I was, I dealt with the press as I thought I should deal with the press as far as the team was concerned, and that wasn't very good PR. I now understand from a journalist's point of view, they've got to get something for tomorrow's paper and I wasn't giving them anything. They go, "Well, fuck him anyway", and it gets antagonistic then.

'They didn't have the background to know what they were talking about. Some lad enters journalism and becomes a soccer reporter, immediately becomes a critic, and his views are now read and he considers them important. But to the pros in the game, their reaction is, "What the fuck does he know about it?" So, contempt would be too strong a word, but I didn't have any respect for their views, and I'd say that came across.

'In lots of ways I would have played the game a bit more, but I've no regrets, because I was true to myself. My feeling was that I deal with the players, I get on extremely well with the players and they are the ones that matter. Players are very sensitive, very insecure people. When you're a manager and you're being true to your players, if you can get away without giving the press anything then you're doing well. But the press are very powerful as well in presenting the image which is very important to the public and the public's reaction then to their team.

'I don't think I've ever been the clever guy that people said I was. I don't consider myself such a clever guy at all. I'm a football man – always have been a football man.'

Chapter Five

MICHAEL, MICK, JIM AND SEAMUS

KATHLEEN ROBINSON would do anything for her son Michael. He could be a selfish, headstrong boy, but he was determined and single-minded. He had carved out a career in football even though his father had often told him he wasn't very good, and he had been a professional footballer himself. All Michael was ever interested in was football. So when he started asking her about her old Irish relatives that she had mentioned from time to time, it puzzled her somewhat. Yes, her grandmother, Eliza Morgan, had been an actress or something, from Cork she thought, and she had come over to tread the boards on the West End. Was Cork in Southern Ireland or Northern Ireland? Southern Ireland. When Michael then said that he could play international football if she gave up her British citizenship and changed her nationality, that puzzled her even more. Despite the derision of his father, Michael had always said he would play for England one day. And nothing would convince him otherwise, even when he came under the wing of the assistant manager at Preston North End, Alan Kelly.

Kelly had been teaching him about football, telling him that as a big centre forward he had to learn to be more aggressive. When I was a goalkeeper, Kelly told him, you wouldn't have scared me. Kelly knew that Michael had some Irish ancestry, and told him that he might be able to play for Ireland. Michael, displaying that all-important streak of aggressiveness, had told him no way, there was only one country he was playing for – and that was England.

And that was the way things were going. He got a call up for the England Under-21 squad but, cruelly, was injured. Mike (Don't call me Mick, it sounds like a dog food), then made his big move. Malcolm Allison came over from Manchester City and paid £750,000 for him. He became the second most expensive player in Britain, and Allison trumpeted that he had bought England's next centre forward. To say that Michael had the world at his feet was an understatement. Now the press were beginning to show an interest. The people from *Shoot!* magazine had contacted him to do a profile. No problem.

He wasn't doing that well at City however. Allison wouldn't play him at centre forward for a start. And this was the First Division, not the Third. He had made the break for the big time too early. By the end of the season Michael was on the way out. He was an embarrassment to Allison. There were talks with Alan Mullery at Brighton and it looked like his time with a glamour club, never mind his England prospects, was coming to an abrupt end. Something was needed to get his career going again. He began to recall what Alan Kelly had said to him about international football and playing for Ireland. And then that *Shoot!* profile that he had done some time back came out:

Make of car: VW Passat
Favourite Food: Steak
Professional Ambition: To play for England

> Person in the world you would most like to meet:
> England manager Ron Greenwood on international
> business.

And there was a picture of Michael sitting at a table eating a whole chicken, dressed in his Manchester City shirt. It was all a bit silly. By the time it was published, Michael was already on his way to Brighton. And forget about England, he was getting more and more interested in playing for Ireland.

He talked to a journalist at the *Sunday World* in Dublin, who ran a piece saying that Michael could play for Ireland. Wouldn't Robinson be the answer to Ireland's perennial striker problem, the author asked. The FAI indicated that their answer was yes. All Michael needed now was to get an Irish passport, or proof that he was eligible for one.

The word from the Irish embassy wasn't good however. Yes, he had Irish blood but he wasn't entitled to a passport. The connection went back too far; his Irish relative was a *great-grandmother*. He would only have been eligible if she had been his *grandmother*. And there were no special cases. Michael was close to despair but, in typical fashion, he refused to give up. Hadn't he cleaned Ray Treacy's boots while an apprentice at Preston, and you can't get more Irish than that. Wasn't there anything the embassy could do? Well, the embassy official said, the person who *is* entitled to an Irish passport in the Robinson family is Michael's mother, Kathleen. If she changes her nationality from British subject to Irish citizen – and there's nothing to stop her – then Michael can too. The footballer clenched his two fists and punched the air in triumph. Michael approached his mother again at the family hotel in Blackpool . . . He was in an unusually serious mood, explaining that there would be a lot of paperwork but it would be worth it in the end. 'For you, son,' Kathleen told him, 'anything.'

Now it was a race against time. Ireland's match against Belgium is only two weeks away. Brendan Menton at the FAI is getting a copy of the great-grandmother's birth certificate from the Registrar of Births and Deaths in Dublin. Right then. Now we can get the Kathleen Robinson passport; but it's already too late for the Belgium game. The next target is a further three weeks away, against France. Okay, passport for Kathleen Robinson comes through. Now it's a formality. Michael can get an Irish passport as well. Bingo! He's been named in the team. Playing up front with Frank Stapleton and Steve Heighway. Out goes Don Givens. Great servant of Ireland down the years. That hat-trick against Russia. Brilliant.

The papers are full of it: FOURTH GENERATION EXILE IS PICKED FOR IRELAND; NEW SON FOR THE OULD SOD; I CAN'T WAIT TO WEAR THE GREEN JERSEY SAYS MICK ROBINSON. Nobody seems to have noticed the *Shoot!* profile, which is a bit of a relief. Or if they have, they haven't said anything. In fact it's time for another one. This time for the Brighton club programme. No problem.

Car: Mazda 626 Coupé
Favourite Food: Steak
Favourite Music: Wolfe Tones, The Dublin City
    Ramblers
Biggest disappointment in life: Not being born in Ireland

★

Michael Robinson got over his disappointment to play 24 times for Ireland, until Jack Charlton gave him the chop. Although an extreme example, he was one of a new breed of players from across the water who would provide that added ingredient to help Ireland eventually break through to the big time. It's not a Charlton phenomenon. When Ireland played Wales in 1981, five years before Jack took over and shortly after Eoin Hand had taken over the manager's job, there were six English-born players on the team – McDonagh, O'Callaghan, Hughton, Grealish, Waddock and O'Keefe. Robinson was to join them shortly afterwards.

Nor is it a granny rule as such; it's just a rule that favours the Irish more than most other countries. Article 18 of FIFA's constitution covering the nationality and eligibility of players states: 'Any person who is a naturalised citizen of a country in virtue of that country's laws shall be eligible to play for a national or representative team of that country.' Ireland's citizenship laws are in one area more liberal than virtually any other country in the world. No matter where a person is born, anyone whose parent or grandparent is an Irish citizen is himself entitled to Irish citizenship. Hence the so-called granny rule.

The FIFA law was introduced after a situation developed in the thirties and forties where players were playing for a number of different countries; the Irish citizenship laws weren't introduced until 1956. Shay Brennan, who played for Manchester United in the sixties, is believed to be the first English-born person to play for Ireland. It is widely assumed that Joe Kinnear is English, but he was born in Kimmage, Dublin, and lived there till he was eleven. There could have been thousands of others in the sixties, but they wouldn't have known about Ireland, and Ireland wouldn't have known about them. The Big Five selection committee, which had few contacts with English clubs and managers, found it difficult enough keeping track of Irish-born players in England. Tony Byrne from Co Laois played for Southampton for years before two *Irish Times* journalists brought him to the attention of the selectors and he was immediately capped.

Under Tuohy's management in the early seventies, an abortive attempt was made to draft in the promising young Charlton Athletic striker, Mick Flanagan, of Essex, whose parents came from Offaly. He was introduced to the FAI by the Charlton manager and former Irish international, Theo Foley. Flanagan was named in the Irish squad for the World Cup game against France but had to withdraw when it was discovered he had played at youth level for England.

It was only when Giles became established as manager that the influx started. Many of these would come through the youth and Under-21 set-up. In 1978 Giles had appointed Eamon Dunphy manager of the youth team. 'We were absolutely desperate for players,' Dunphy said, 'and we used our contacts in England to try to strengthen the squad.' One of these was Bob Hennessy, a Dublin journalist who had moved to London to work for the Press Association racing team and was also sending snippets about soccer back to the Irish papers. Hennessy was as much an unofficial minder to the Irish team as he was a journalist. A youth team player, Ronnie Whelan, stayed in his house when he came to London from Liverpool to meet up with the squad and found he had no hotel accommodation. As one of the few Irish sports journalists working in England, Hennessy had built up a hefty contacts book of players involved with Ireland at all levels. When a young player moved clubs or moved in with another landlady, Hennessy would assiduously track their movements.

'I would find out about a player with Irish connections and then I'd knock off a letter to Dunphy or Gilesy: "Did you know that guy? He must be one of ours." Next thing you'd see his name in the squad. The FAI in Merrion Square would not be aware that this guy existed and generally we had a tendency to say, "Quick, grab him." Suddenly there would be an O'Shaughnessy in the Irish youth squad. People at home would think, "Who the hell is he?" and I'd have found out that his father was a taxi-driver in Coventry and was Dublin-born.'

Though Giles didn't actively go seeking them out, he had no qualms about picking English-born players. 'I would have picked anybody. I would have loved to have gone with a full Irish team, but if I had the players who were good enough and qualified for me then I would pick them.'

A difference in reaction from the crowd to these players was noted by Giles. 'It was typically Irish, wasn't it? If it was an English guy they took to him straight away. It was the old Irish inferiority complex. Here was somebody who was English playing for us. They must be good if they have an English accent. That used to drive me mad because I felt we could do it, but if somebody had an English accent they were much better received.'

Giles' most valuable recruit was the central defender Mark Lawrenson, who would subsequently always be referred to in British footballing circles as the Irish player who could have played for England. That he didn't was largely thanks to his mother, Theresa Crotty, who wasn't sure that she wanted him to play football at all. Theresa Crotty's father moved his wife and six children from their home in Waterford to take up a job as a foreman with a construction company in Preston. The move came in the early fifties – a time when thousands of Irish people were coming to England to find work in the post-war construction boom. Having spent her teenage years in the north-west of England, Theresa Crotty married Tommy Lawrenson, a professional footballer at Preston. Their son Mark always wanted to follow in his father's footsteps, but his mother wanted him to complete his O-levels and A-levels. As a result Mark matured late – he was compared at the age of 16 to a new-born foal – and there were only hints of his immense talent by the time he made his debut for Preston at the age of 17. Again, Alan Kelly, who was also assistant manager with Ireland and was another Giles brother-in-law, was waiting to pounce.

Lawrenson had started at Preston as a left-winger but had blossomed when switched to the back four. As with Robinson, Kelly knew of Lawrenson's Irish connections and asked him would he be interested in playing for Ireland. It was something that hadn't even occurred to Lawrenson. 'I grew up in England, basically, and I suppose I considered myself English. I had been to Ireland a couple of times but I had no great conception about the country. I'd followed their results purely because I knew Alan Kelly and Ray Treacy.

'I suppose the first thing I thought was, "What's the alternative?" And the alternative was to play for England. And I said to myself, "I don't think that realistically will be an alternative." When you talk to an 18-year-old, spotty-faced kid playing in the middle of the Third Division and someone asks if you would like to play international football, the answer is going to be "Yeah".'

Lawrenson had also turned for advice to another formidable figure, the Preston manager and yet another of Giles' brothers-in-law, Nobby Stiles. 'Nobby told me that if anybody was going to turn the whole thing round and turn Ireland into a professional outfit, it would be Johnny Giles. So I thought, "Yeah, let's go and give it a go".'

Lawrenson wasn't just an unknown quantity for England. When he made his debut at the age of 19 in a friendly game against Poland in 1977, Giles had picked him without having seen him play.

As manager of West Brom, Giles had been watching Laurie Cunningham at Leyton Orient. He also used the opportunity to assess the international prospects of a 17-year-old London boy, Tony Grealish. For Grealish, even then, Leyton Stadium in east London was a small stage – he already held the distinction of playing at both Wembley and Croke Park as a Gaelic footballer. Grealish had an idyllic London-Irish upbringing. His parents, Packie and Nora, met in London after both emigrating from Ireland in the fifties. They married and settled in a big council house in West Kilburn. Together they ran the St Gabriel's hurling team at the Gaelic Athletic Association complex at New Eltham in east London. Every Sunday, the Grealish family would go to Mass, come home, where the boys would wash the Brylcreem from their hair, and then go to New Eltham for the day. Tony and his brother Brian excelled at Gaelic football and on big match days for both the hurling and the Gaelic football, a coach would come to pick them up at their home.

'About nine of the players and their families would be on the coach,' Grealish says. 'Up and down the street people would be looking on to see what was going on. They couldn't get over the fact that these lads were arriving with sticks and boots hanging over their shoulders. There'd be a big gang of people outside with kids and everything. They'd be having a fag and kidding and messing around.'

The Grealish home was always an important stopping point. As well as Tony and Brian, at the house there would usually be a couple of cousins from Ireland who had come over to work for a year and were also involved in the Gaelic. The boys would practise their playing skills in a field near the house, with their English friends looking on in amazement. 'A lot of me friends used to think it was a crazy game, especially the hurling, they couldn't get over that, this stick shaped like a rifle, and the lads smashing the *sliotar* against each other. They'd be saying, "These mad Paddys." Afterwards we used to get the ball and throw it to them and it would sting their hands. There would be two or three black guys there and it always amused me to see them pick up the hurley and have a go.'

At the age of 14 Grealish played Gaelic at Wembley at junior level before an exhibition game between London and Kerry. 'We thought that was vast until we went to play at Croke Park. I just couldn't get over the size of the pitch.' London were the 33rd county in the All-Ireland Minor Football Championship. They played Cavan in the quarter-final and were beaten by two points.

Unlike many of his contemporaries in Ireland, Grealish's prowess on the Gaelic field didn't prevent him pursuing his interest in soccer. Whereas soccer would have been banned as an organised sport in many Irish schools because it was regarded as an English game, Grealish could pursue both his interests with impunity. His weekends were crammed with sport; school soccer on Saturday, club soccer on Sunday mornings and then over to New Eltham on the Sunday afternoon for Gaelic football. The weekend evenings would also reflect the differing influence on his life. The place to go to was the National Ballroom in Kilburn, where there was an Irish showband in one huge hall and a disco in a smaller part where the younger people gathered, and the night would end with the playing of the Irish national anthem.

At the age of 16, Grealish left school and joined Leyton Orient as an apprentice. He was picked to go on trial with the

English youth team at Lilleshall and played in several non-representative matches for them with players such as Glen Hoddle and Ray Wilkins against Under-21 club sides. He believes his conversion to the Irish side came when a press photographer who covered the Gaelic football scene in London alerted the FAI. Grealish was approached by John Jarman, the then Irish youth team coach, and was selected to play in a youth championship game against England in Switzerland.

'I walked out on to the pitch and met all the lads I'd been playing with and training with on the English side. Alan Curbishley said to me, "What are you joining them Paddies for?" They couldn't understand why I was getting mixed up with the Irish side because we were like the poor relations, we had skimpy old tracksuits. But they didn't know where I was coming from.'

Though won over to the Irish, Grealish was shortly to be lost to Gaelic games. At the age of 20, while still playing at New Eltham on the Sunday afternoon, he was approached by his manager at Orient, George Petchey. 'He said, "You've got to knock this on the head, especially the hurling, let alone the Gaelic football, because you're in the first team now, you're playing two days a week".' Petchey laid it on the line for the young Grealish: 'All those mad fuckers can do what they like, but you're not playing with them.'

While Grealish effortlessly evolved from a junior Gaelic star into a young professional footballer, up in Rotherham, Yorkshire, Seamus McDonagh was struggling to make sense of his Irish roots. His Irish parents, Mick and Angie, had met at a dance in Leicester; his father had worked as a navvy and then down the coalmines in Rotherham. But he then deserted the family home leaving Angie to bring up their four children on her own. His mother's reluctance to talk about the past left her sensitive son struggling to work it out for himself. 'We'd go back to Tipperary where me mother's from and we'd be playing with the Irish kids; you'd be English, yet in England, where we were born all four of us, we were Irish; Irish name, Catholics, we were different, we were Irish. That was a real eye-opener.'

McDonagh's name didn't help. He was baptised James Martin Seamus (the Irish for James) McDonagh, but everybody called him Seamus, except his teacher Mrs Higgins. 'Mrs Higgins' class; I'd be ten. I was in the back of the class, the last desk on my own. Mrs Higgins, she was a real hard one, God rest her soul. She said, I'll never forget this, "James, come out here please. James, come out here." Then she pointed at me. I said, "Excuse me, miss, I'm Seamus." And she said, "Stupid boy." I had to come up in front of the class and see that my name was "James" on the register. Ashamed, I was, in class.

'Growing up in England you'd got this thing that the Irish were thick and drinkers. You kind of thought that yourself. You'd see these fellas drinking or drunk in the street and you would look down on them, because you grew up in England and you were ashamed. And then when you got enlightenment and started reading books, they'd got some of the best writers in the world, they gave the world some of the best minds and scholars.

'I always read about Ireland. I loved history at school and geography. I would read a few historical Irish novels like *The Scorching Wind* by Walter Macken. I was fascinated by the turn of the century – Maud Gonne, Yeats, McBride and all that. I think if I could have been alive in another life, I'd love to have been alive at the turn of the century. That time and leading up to the 1916 rising, which wasn't romantic at all.

'When I was 16 and I had just signed as an apprentice at Rotherham I remember I was going to Mass and this guy Meehan said to me, "You qualify to play for Ireland, you know." I was surprised because I hadn't thought about any international football. Then at 17, I was coming on and people were watching me. I got picked to go to Lilleshall for a youth trial for England. Then I got picked for the squad. We went to Spain, and I came on as a sub, so in theory I was capped, but that apparently didn't bar me from playing for Ireland.

'When I went to Bolton Wanderers, Tony Dunne told the FAI about me, but they took it no further. It was only when I went to Everton and the secretary, Jim Greenwood, told me I was eligible that it was sorted out. Eoin Hand came over to watch me and I recited to him the proclamation from the Easter Rising: "Irishmen and Irish women, in the name of God and of the dead generations from which she receives her old tradition of nationhood, Ireland, through us, summons her children to her flag and strikes for her freedom . . ." He thought I was mad actually. He asked Steve McMahon who said he wanted to play for England. His grandparents were Irish but he saw himself as an English boy. My team-mates just thought I was getting a cap through the back door because I wasn't going to get picked for England.

'I went over on the boat, it was symbolic of going back, the boat. We were playing Wales at Tolka Park. I never slept, I had a nightmare. Eoin was talking to me, saying he had got a bit of stick for bringing this English kid over, because he had given me a big build-up. The Welsh manager, Mike England, had made a complaint about these Englishmen being dug up to play for Ireland.

'I met Liam Brady and he thought I had just jumped on the bandwagon, you couldn't convince him otherwise. He said you played for England youth and were delighted to do that. It used to upset me when people thought I'd changed my name because I'd played for Ireland. But it had always been Jim or Seamus at the clubs. The manager at Bolton had said to me, "Is your name Jim or Seamus?" I said, "It's Seamus." "Right," he said, "I'll call you Jim." He was taking the piss, because a lot of people in England can't say Seamus.'

Ireland went into the qualifying campaign for the 1982 World Cup campaign with its strongest ever squad. As well as that interesting bunch of characters from England, three lads from North Dublin, David O'Leary, Frank Stapleton and Brady, were now being talked about as being among the best in their positions in Europe. Following Giles' resignation, the FAI had turned to Alan Kelly, who had replaced Nobby Stiles as manager at Preston. He had been appointed caretaker manager

As Ireland's new manager, John Giles saw his main task as destroying the culture of the moral victory (Sunday Independent)

Liam Tuohy, one of Ireland's first 'real' managers, who found his niche in charge of the youths, but his experiences with Charlton ended in bitter recriminations on both sides (Sunday Independent)

Liam Brady was unstoppable when he turned it on for Ireland
(Sunday Independent)

Eamon Dunphy enjoying the good life as a member of the Irish soccer writers'
fraternity. He had Eoin Hand for starters but Charlton repeated on him
(Sunday Independent)

Eoin Hand's determination to cling on to his job meant he paid a heavy personal price for failure (Sunday Independent)

Field of dreams: John Giles said he could bring European cups to Shamrock Rovers, but a few years later his dreams, and Glenmalure Park itself, lay in ruins
(Sunday Independent)

Michael Robinson's dream had always been to play for England, but nobody went to such great efforts to pull on the green shirt (Sunday Independent)

Chelsea footballer Vinnie Jones, with the help of Bid Doyle, executive officer of the General Registrar Office in Dublin, looks for the Irish roots which would allow him to qualify to play for Ireland

The committee room where Charlton's fraught election took place

Charlton gradually began to win respect and Jim Cogan's cartoon in 1987
portrayed him as the man holding up the crumbling edifice of the FAI
(Sunday Independent)

Mick McCarthy put to the test by Marco van Basten in the European Championships (Sunday Independent)

Charlton and Stapleton fell out over money, Stapleton's place in the team and wearing hats in the sun (Sunday Independent)

Charlton and Bingham have a frank exchange of views on mercenaries and the diaspora (Billy Stickland, Inpho)

of Ireland, and was being offered a two-year contract, but his club objected to this and Kelly chose to remain at Preston. Kelly's assistant, Eoin Hand, then took over in a caretaker capacity for a home game against Argentina, which the World Champions won 1-0. Hand's name then went into the ring with a number of other Irish-based candidates and, after a series of interviews at the Burlington Hotel, he was offered a two-year contract.

Hand was a former Irish international who had spent most of his playing career as a centre back at Portsmouth and was now managing Limerick United. At 34, he was a novice at management level, and had made a promising start by guiding Limerick United to the League of Ireland championship in his first season. His transition to international football management also appeared to bode well. Ireland, playing attacking, entertaining football, beat Holland in their second qualifying game for the 1982 World Cup. They also beat France and Cyprus at home, drew away to Holland but were beaten in France and were doomed to lose in Belgium. Ireland lost out on goal difference to France, but it was the most concerted effort so far to qualify.

The campaign also marked a significant triumph for the FAI administrators. Ever since Irish players started playing in the English Leagues, clubs had enjoyed the privilege of preventing them playing for their country in the event of a clash of fixtures. In this case, several English clubs had refused to release their Irish players for the game in Paris as there was a group of League Cup matches on the same night. The FAI acted quickly and appealed successfully to UEFA for the release of players under legislation introduced a year earlier giving priority to competitive international fixtures.

That breakthrough aside, the FAI, after the appointment of Hand, renewed its licence to behave in a fashion hostile to producing good results. A trip was organised for friendly games against Poland and a West Germany B team – and it seemed like a harbinger for a return to the good old days.

Firstly the officials questioned the make-up of Hand's squad, his first for an away tour. They were unhappy with two players, but Hand refused to back down and he went on the trip with his chosen squad.

The game against the West German B team passed off without hitch, other than a 0-3 defeat. The next stop was Poland, a country in turmoil as Solidarity locked horns with the Soviet puppet government of General Jaruzelski. The venue for the game was in a town called Bydgoszcz, about 300 kilometres west of Warsaw, but a rump of the party never made the match. 'A group of the officials jumped off the coach at a big hotel in Warsaw,' says Mark Lawrenson. 'All with big bright eyes, saying "See you later, boys." That last impression was imprinted on our brains.'

It wasn't so much a coach as a van used by road labourers, and it bumped its way to Bydgoszcz over a five-hour journey. The players arrived at their destination weary, hungry and unhappy. With two days to kill before the game, their sense of gloom deepened when they got to their hotel. 'The hotel, or what was classed as a hotel, was dirty,' says Lawrenson. 'There were no towels, no toilet paper, stuff like that.' Food, judging from the long bread queues that the players had witnessed as they drove into the town, was also going to be a problem. 'The thinking in those days was that you had steak the day before the game. The steak turned out to be hamburger, but it was the best the Poles could find.'

There was little the players could do. Hand decided he should let the players go out for a few beers to lighten their troubles. 'It wasn't the manager's fault,' Lawrenson says, 'it wasn't the hotel's fault, it was the fault of somebody in a five-star hotel 200 miles away, lording it up. That was the first time I saw the players in danger of revolting and saying we weren't going to play. The secretary, Peader O'Driscoll, waltzed into the hotel on the day of the game and we just went nuts at him. We told him that if our clubs knew exactly what we'd gone through, most of us would possibly not get released again.'

Poland dominated the game, forcing Pat Bonner of Glasgow Celtic to pick the ball out of the net three times on his international debut. Afterwards, an official Polish FA car was attacked by supporters after they saw the number plates, but the Irish officials inside it, those who had actually travelled with the players and attended the game, escaped unscathed. The players demanded to be returned to Warsaw that evening, and stepped back on their coach. Several were ill on the way back to the capital and had to use the embroidered napkins given to them as a gesture of its hospitality by the Polish FA. The scene that greeted them back at the hotel in Warsaw where most of the officials had remained was like something out of a saucy seaside revue. The players had a few more drinks and enjoyed the show.

Though several journalists were on the Polish trip, the team's experiences off the pitch weren't known about at the time. Noel Dunne in the *Irish Independent* commented that, 'this sudden slump by the Irish side back into the dark ages of football is quite baffling'. And the performance of the team in getting to within a hair's breadth of qualification for the 1982 World Cup acted as a panacea for the FAI's ills. But the next tour abroad was to expose the FAI's incompetence to the full glare of publicity and would mark the end of Eoin Hand's honeymoon period as Irish manager.

The FAI had lined up another tour of South America, this time against Argentina, Chile and Brazil. The tour was scheduled to begin in the early summer of 1982 and, unfettered by any UEFA regulations, it was clear that several top clubs would not be releasing their Irish players as they had league or tour commitments. The FAI would still have been able to muster a respectable squad, but its plans were thrown into disarray when Argentina took over the Falkland Islands at the beginning of April. Ireland's first match was due to be played against Argentina on 18 May and the whole tour was now in jeopardy. In war, if truth is the first casualty then sport is often a close second. The British Government, having dispatched her navy to try to recover the islands, called for the cancellation of all sports fixtures between Britain and Argentina. Theoretically, this had nothing to do with Ireland, but it quickly became obvious that not a single English club would be releasing their Irish players for the tour unless the match against Argentina was called off.

The Falklands affair touched a sensitive nerve in Ireland, a country whose political make-up had been shaped by Britain's colonial history. Though the Republic was a neutral country, it had rowed along with economic sanctions introduced by the European Community against Argentina, but there was a strong debate in the country about Britain's right to recover the islands. The action of the English clubs in banning Irish players from travelling to Argentina was pounced on by some of Britain's critics and pressure was put on the FAI to meet its tour commitments at any cost.

'Even if the FAI have to reach down to junior level to make up a squad, they should send a team to Argentina,' said one prominent member of the governing Fianna Fail party, Niall Andrews. 'We are not at war with Argentina and we shouldn't be governed by the managers of British soccer teams as to who, how and when we play.'

One option was to send a team from the League of Ireland – but this was not an attractive one. The previous year a League of Ireland team had been beaten 6-0 in Brazil and the host nation had been angry about the imbalance between the two sides. What's more the League of Ireland was committed to sending a team to New Zealand for another tour, so only the equivalent of a League of Ireland B team could be sent to South America.

With pressure on it from all sides the FAI equivocated, hoping the problem would simply go away. There was also a financial imperative, as a fixture against the reigning world champions in the River Plate Stadium would be a lucrative one. In early May, with the tour still two weeks away, the FAI announced that the match against Argentina would go ahead and that it expected the English clubs to release the players.

Predictably, the FAI was ignored. A week later, with the date of departure only a few days away, the FAI performed a U-turn, and announced, as the British clubs had demanded a month ago, that the match against Argentina would be called off. Eoin Hand was dispatched to Britain on his own mission of shuttle diplomacy in a late effort to secure the release of players.

Brighton and Hove Albion said it would release three of its players, but Manchester United and Arsenal, who between them had five senior internationals, announced they were bringing the players off on their own tours. Eoin Hand went to see Bob Paisley at Anfield to see if he could secure the release of Kevin Sheedy, Ronnie Whelan and Mark Lawrenson. Hand was in a hopeless position.

'The club advised us not to go, for our safety as much as anything else. I suppose they had visions of us not coming back,' Lawrenson says. 'We'd had had a long season and I could see what was going to happen. The Brazilian game had three different venues within a week. First it was the Maracana stadium, then it was Sao Paolo, then it was somewhere else. So we didn't go. I think we read it right.'

The Irish squad flew from London to Madrid and then boarded an Iberia Airlines flight. 'I took a sleeping tablet, 'cos I hate those long flights,' Seamus McDonagh says. 'I woke up and it was morning and we were preparing to land. I looked out the window expecting to see Santiago, and I see this sign saying "Aeroporto Buenos Aires". I can't believe it, because the Falklands War is on and people have been killed.'

The plane was in Buenos Aires on a stop-over to Chile, and Argentinian soldiers came on board to inspect passports. 'A lot of the lads had British passports and there was some trouble over that,' says Tony Grealish. The players were taken off the plane and were put in a room with a couple of young soldiers. Gerry Daly lit up a cigarette and shouted to one of them: 'Can we have some sandwiches in here, and coffee?' A soldier muttered an oath about the English, and Daly shouted back, 'We're fucking Irish, Irish.' Meanwhile, Eoin Hand and the accompanying FAI officials had managed to convince the airport authorities of their Irish *bona fides* and the atmosphere at the airport changed from one of mutual suspicion to one of fraternity. The squad was given permission to continue on its way. Sandwiches and tea were brought for the party and consumed back on the plane. 'We were worried at the time because of the political situation, but I thought they treated us very well,' says Daly. 'It wasn't a problem for them that Ireland was only 50 or 60 miles across the water from England.'

In Santiago, the footballing omens for the tour were writ large when Gamboa scored for Chile in the first minute of Ireland's first match. There then followed a 7-0 hammering at the hands of Brazil in Uberlandia. The FAI had arranged at the last minute that as a substitute for the Argentinian game, the tour would end with a visit to the Caribbean and a game against Trinidad and Tobago. After the Brazilian game several of the players threatened to go straight home, but agreed to continue after receiving their one-thousand dollar payment for the trip. They had a party in Rio rather than pack it in.

However, Brady who had shown his good faith by being the first big name to make himself available for the tour, had had enough. Humiliated and upset after the Brazilian game – where he had been the star attraction for the local crowd – he announced that he was returning to Italy, even if he had to pay his own fare. Rather than being on a trip that was a shambles he should be at home with his wife celebrating their first wedding anniversary. Brady also had important business in Italy involving the negotiation of his transfer from Juventus to Sampdoria and his professional stature hadn't been improved by the calamity he had become involved in with the international side. The squad left for Trinidad without him, but the assistant manager, Terry Conroy, stayed behind with Brady. The next day he agreed to follow the squad to Trinidad. Brazil had been Ireland's heaviest ever defeat, but Trinidad and Tobago was to be the most humiliating. Ireland lost the match 2-1.

After the tour, Hand vowed he would never lead the team

into such a debacle again. He was a hard-working and conscientious manager; unlike Giles, he assiduously checked on the form of his players, going across to England virtually every week in the season to attend games. Hand travelled constantly, vetting opposition sides or attending competitions that Ireland hadn't qualified for. For a World Cup game against the Soviet Union in Moscow, Hand arranged for the food to be brought over from Ireland and his wife came along to do the cooking. The FAI, dismayed at the expense and baffled by the manager's enthusiasm, were slow to support Hand in his work. In his book *The Eoin Hand Story*, he described arriving at Merrion Square to discuss arrangements for a trip abroad with the Secretary, Peadar O'Driscoll, and the Honorary Treasurer, Charlie Walsh. Instead, the two officials argued furiously about the composition of the FAI travelling party and then stormed off.

Despite the enthusiasm, Hand cut a sorry figure as he went from country to country. He describes going to the European Championships in 1980 in Italy and arriving at the San Siro stadium to pick up his ticket. None was waiting for him and a journalist had to get him into the match. The same happened in Rome. 'In both Milan and Rome, the hotel accommodation booked left a lot to be desired,' Hand writes. 'In both cities I was ashamed to let anyone see me enter or leave as I felt it would reflect badly on the country.' In the World Cup in Spain in 1982 Hand stayed with a number of Irish journalists in an apartment in Madrid and had to ring Ron Greenwood, the English manager, to get tickets for games.

However, Hand took pride in the fact that, at the age of 34, he was the youngest manager in Europe, if not the world. He also attended managerial conferences in Split, Yugoslavia, and liked to compare himself to his managerial colleagues in Britain at the time, Ron Greenwood and Alex Ferguson and to the Northern Ireland manager, Billy Bingham. But unlike them he had still to establish a pedigree and assert himself as manager. John Giles had commented when his successors came into the job that of all the players in his squad, the two he could least imagine going into management were Eoin Hand and Terry Conroy. As a player, Hand was an enthusiastic if unexceptional centre back who spent years of toil in the lower divisions of the English leagues. Making the leap to international management, he found it difficult to portray himself as an authoritative figure to players whose achievements were greater than his.

'Eoin was probably not forceful enough,' Frank Stapleton said later in an interview in *Hot Press*. 'I think he kind of felt a little, I'm looking for the word, a little bit overawed.'

'The players liked him, they wanted to play for him,' says Mark Lawrenson. 'I just think tactically at that level he was somewhat naïve. We thought it was probably better to go away and have people say "Oh, what a lovely team they are. Weren't they unlucky?" As opposed to going away and getting a draw and then beating them at home.'

The centre half at Manchester City, Mick McCarthy, was brought into the squad by Hand: 'Eoin used to run a happy ship,' McCarthy says, 'and everybody used to enjoy coming over. If anything, the problem was with handling star names. The fact that some of the names were actually bigger than the team. I remember it was very difficult for him to criticise the likes of Liam, Dave O'Leary, Mark Lawrenson, Frank Stapleton, Gerry Daly. Maybe the mutual respect wasn't there for Eoin because he was not as successful as a player as they had been. That's the opinion I got at the time.'

After Trinidad and Tobago, Ireland's next match also ended in a 2-1 defeat, away to Holland in the opening game of the qualifying round of the European Championships. Hand was criticised for playing Mark Lawrenson at right back and persevering with Tony Grealish and Gerry Daly in midfield instead of introducing some younger blood. In the next away games Ireland managed a 1-0 victory over Malta and were beaten 2-0 by Spain, where Hand's defensive formation baffled some of his players. Ashley Grimes of Manchester United threw his boot in Hand's direction on being substituted and rarely got the chance to play for Ireland again. On the plane on the way back from Zaragoza, some drunken supporters travelling with the team chanted for Hand's dismissal. Ireland beat Iceland 3-0 away, but then in an undisciplined performance, conceded three late goals to lose 3-2 at home to Holland. They were out of the Championships.

It had been a poor campaign and the following month, November 1983, the FAI Executive met to consider Hand's position. The meeting was called for three p.m. and Hand was invited to attend at four p.m. Before his arrival, one member of the Executive, Tony O'Neill, called for a completely new approach to our international team. He said the FAI should look at new candidates and consider paying up to IR£30,000 per annum to a suitably qualified person. The FAI President, John Farrell, pointed out that Eoin Hand had built up a good squad of players and had excellent connections with English club managers. The Honorary Treasurer, Charlie Walsh, said that if Mr Hand's contract was terminated, it would involve the Association in a heavy financial commitment. Pat O'Brien said that it had been implied that our international players were dictating the style of play to the manager.

Hand then attended the meeting. In reply to remarks about 'player power' he said he would resign rather than have pressure put on him by the players. Hand said the FAI were very helpful when a problem came up. He said he had no problems with administration and the current arrangements were first-class. Hand then left the meeting. A motion that Hand be reappointed until the last match of the World Cup 1986 was carried by nine votes to three.

Ireland in their next match were beaten 3-0 in a friendly away to Israel – and a home game against Mexico drew a crowd of only 6,000 to Dalymount Park, the lowest ever attendance for a Republic of Ireland home game.

The slump in Ireland's fortunes was the signal for a furious attack on the FAI and Eoin Hand by Eamon Dunphy. After hanging up his boots, Dunphy had decided on a career in sports journalism, where he was about to make a far greater impact than he had on the pitch. Dunphy had started hanging around with the press pack and drinking with the manager and FAI officials. His dim view of the set-up when a player had only been reconfirmed as he approached it from a different angle ten years on.

Dunphy takes his football very seriously: 'Really without children, without dreams, without fans, football is just another way of spending time, wasting time. Its real force in society, its value to the culture is the richness of the relationship between people's imaginings and dreams and the game itself.' He was incensed that others didn't seem to share this passion. 'I was the first sports writer here to take the job seriously, and it was very difficult. I was 34, I had given up football and I was immediately writing about friends of mine. I grew up with Eoin Hand, we were on the same street together, we went to the same picture houses, we screwed the same birds. I knew Eoin. I didn't dislike him at all. But I had to lay that aside. I was working for my newspaper and therefore my readers.

'They were desperate times. What was really desperate about them was that we had the makings of a really good side. There was this awful sense that a historic opportunity was being missed because he was a compliant and pliable fellow and a clubbable guy who was inoffensive. He liked a pint, knew all the press.'

Dunphy's campaign wasn't just against Hand, it was against what he called Decentskinsmanship. He defined this as a conspiracy of silence between bad administrators, complacent journalists and broadcasters and those within the game, players and managers, who are less than brilliant at their jobs. To be a Decent Skin, Dunphy said, is to overlook the shortcomings of those with whom you travel and associate on the grounds that (a) we are in this together and (b) the public won't know any different anyway. Week after week, in his column in the *Sunday Tribune*, Dunphy attacked the administrators and the manager. He also turned his fury on the two most influential and highly rated players in the team, the playmaker Liam Brady and the captain Frank Stapleton.

Brady was a powerful figure in the Irish set-up, whose influence extended beyond the playing field. In 1985, Brady was due to win his 50th cap in a game against Norway, but this wasn't considered a fitting setting for such an important milestone. One of Brady's first appearances in the green shirt had been in a representative game against a West German B team ten years previously. The FAI, creating nightmares for the statisticians, upgraded this game to a full international, thus allowing Brady to win his 50th cap against England in the glamorous surroundings of Wembley stadium. On the field, Brady had clear ideas about his role in the Irish side which Hand went along with, but his performances in the Irish shirt had been patchy at best. Dunphy, going for the jugular, described Brady as 'rich promise turned to sulky self-indulgence' and 'a parody of a player of substance, the triumph of reputation over reality'. Two years previously Dunphy had been in raptures about Stapleton, describing his performance in one game against France as 'a personal triumph, but more profoundly a parable to the magnificence of the human spirit.' Now, Stapleton was an example of 'talent without values'.

Typically, Dunphy's comments caused a strong public reaction. Terry Conroy, Ireland's assistant manager at the time, believes they were even responsible for the fall of Hand. 'People couldn't wait for the articles to come out on a Sunday. And each Sunday he was churning out the same message every time. Then the ordinary fella that went to the matches started quoting ad lib Dunphy: "We're not strong enough in certain areas of the field where we should be." And they started to get technical, to become technical experts on our play. Dunphy's criticism wasn't constructive, it was destructive. He had got the knife into Eoin. Now that, I think, was the downfall of Eoin because if he hadn't lived in Ireland, the pressure wouldn't have got to him. And the pressure did get to him in the last year.'

Hand had been spat at by Shamrock Rovers supporters at Milltown. He was receiving crank phone calls. At school, his children had been attacked and their bicycles vandalised after

Ireland had lost games. 'He was a prisoner in his own town, he couldn't go out to a place where he could feel that people wouldn't have a go at him,' Conroy says. 'And only because of the campaign that Eamon ran against him. The other reporters who were writing at the time would criticise Eoin, but they would never go down to a personal level.'

Ireland had made a bright start to the 1986 World Cup campaign by beating the Soviet Union 1-0 at Lansdowne Road, but then had slumped to a calamitous 0-1 defeat away to Norway, then a part-time professional side. Hand had been heavily criticised after that game for picking Frank Stapleton, who was recovering from injury at the time and wasn't playing first team football for Manchester United. Ireland had also been hammered 3-0 away to Denmark. Hostility towards the team had never been higher by the time Norway came for the return game in Dublin. Hand and his lieutenants were close to breaking point.

'Brady was as white as a sheet before the game,' says right back David Langan, who earned his 16th cap that day. 'He wanted to do well, and everything depended on Liam, and I think it was just getting to him a bit.' The game finished 0-0, with the Irish side a shapeless mess at the end. The crowd chanted, "What a load of rubbish." Behind closed doors in the dressing-room after the match Hand was distraught, complaining about the crowd and how he would be slaughtered by the press. Brady, who had been substituted during the game, told Hand to pull himself together and stop going on about the press and the crowd. Hand then announced that he was resigning, but the players persuaded him to change his mind. The players said they too had to accept the blame for the performance and, if the manager resigned, the FAI would be let off the hook. Afterwards, oranges and bananas were thrown at the players by a group of disgruntled supporters and they heard the old refrain: 'Fuck off back to England.'

The following six months were wretched ones for Republic of Ireland football. With four games still left in the qualifying round, the Republic's chance of making the World Cup had virtually disappeared. The opportunity to get a new manager appointed quickly so as to renew public interest was lost by the stand-off between Hand and the FAI, with one determined to stay on till the end of his contract and the other unwilling to pay the price of having him sacked.

Ireland played their two games against Switzerland, winning 3-0 at home and drawing away. Ireland then lost 2-0 against the Soviet Union in Moscow and ended the campaign by losing 4-1 at home to Denmark. Only 15,000 attended that match, many of them Danes celebrating their team's qualification for the World Cup in Mexico. For some comfort, the Republic's fans looked to the result from Wembley, where Northern Ireland had qualified for their second World Cup in a row by drawing 0-0 with England.

Chapter Six

THE FOURTH MAN

AN IMPOSSIBLY LARGE NUMBER of people in the FAI want to take the credit for bringing Jack Charlton over to Ireland. They can shelter behind the fact that the election of Charlton was by a secret ballot. But the results show that Charlton was the first choice of only three of the 18 members of the FAI executive. And furthermore, as Charlton went up for election, senior officials in the organisation scrambled to introduce the manager with the most successful club record in English football history to run against him. It was high farce, but it was also undoubtedly the FAI's finest hour.

★

The disarray around Lansdowne Road following the surrender to Denmark was nothing compared to the consternation in the FAI offices on the Georgian terraces of Merrion Square. With money from match fixtures being the only source of income,

Irish soccer was going broke. FAI lawyers had even begun investigating the question of liability of the individual members of council should it not be able to pay its way.

The honorary treasurer, Charlie Walsh, had reported losses for the last two seasons of 1984 and 1985 of IR£60,000 and IR£30,000. The situation, said one of the FAI patrons, Frank Davis, was a disgrace. At a council meeting, he complained that IR£23,000 had been spent on a trip to Israel that was, as he put it, only a holiday. The Vice-President, Pat O'Brien, said that IR£13,000 had been lost on a friendly match at home to Poland, and the Honorary Treasurer was anxious to play the fixture away. Walsh himself was downbeat; if a forthcoming lottery wasn't successful, he said, we can close up Merrion Square.

It wasn't the ideal environment in which to go about the appointment of a new manager. A week after the Denmark game, the beleaguered FAI Executive Committee met at Merrion Square. Its members complained about the bad image of the FAI being presented by the media and there was alarm that some of the Committee were leaking items to the press. The meeting then focused on the manager's job. One junior administrator, Michael Hyland, said the manager should be based in England. He was supported by another of the more dynamic FAI officials, Tony O'Neill. 'The talk on the executive was that in order to make things really happen, now we had a team of professional First Division players, we should get a full-time professional manager, whatever his nationality. We had tended to look towards our ex-players such as John, Eoin, Alan Kelly and Liam Tuohy. We felt it was time to come into a new age,' O'Neill says.

The Committee decided to place an advertisement for the post in the British and Irish press; it would not specify whether the manager's job was full or part-time. Hyland proposed that the President, Des Casey and Tony O'Neill would then travel to England together to interview applicants, if there were any. The advertisement appeared in the December issue of UEFA's official bulletin: 'The Football Association of Ireland is seeking the services of a manager/coach for their national team. Must speak English, preferably based in United Kingdom. Apply in writing, stating previous experience to: The General Secretary, FAI, 80 Merrion Square, Dublin 2, Republic of Ireland.'

There was, in fact, an encouraging response to the advertisement. The FAI had also contacted a number of people personally after studying a dossier of potential international managers drawn up by the Director of Coaching, an Englishman, Alan Wade. And so, when O'Neill and Casey set off for England in early December 1985 there were nine people they wanted to see.

Their stop-over in Birmingham looked potentially like the most productive one. At Birmingham airport they had a meeting with John Giles, who was back living in the English Midlands. Giles' career had gone into a tailspin since he had resigned as Irish manager five years previously. The great experiment at Shamrock Rovers had petered out. Besides winning the FAI Cup in his first season, the team had struggled in the League. 'Every game against Shamrock Rovers was like a cup final,' says Noel King, a former Rovers player and manager. 'And you had Dunphy and Giles in midfield, both at the end of their careers, against young players desperate to prove themselves.' The pitch at Milltown was transformed into the best playing surface in the country but, after initial enthusiasm, attendances began sinking back to the pre-Giles days. Many fans were dismayed by Giles' insistence on building play slowly from the back. During one match, a section of the crowd in the terraces turned their backs to watch a rugby game in a nearby field. Giles refused to change his style of play away from home, and Rovers often struggled on muddy pitches. Relations between Giles and the Kilcoynes, who owned Rovers, also soured over the cost of a house which they had built for Giles. He put out a young team, but the apprenticeship scheme central to Giles' long-term plan had floundered because of a lack of funds.

In his later years with Rovers, Giles would leave before the season was finished to coach Vancouver Whitecaps for the summer. In 1983 he resigned and went to live in Canada. However, relations with a new owner of the club, Bob Carter, soured. The two men were incompatible. The transfer of Pierce O'Leary — David's brother — from Shamrock Rovers to Vancouver Whitecaps became an issue between Carter and Giles. Under his agreement with the Kilcoynes, Giles, while still at Rovers, had received 20 per cent of the transfer fee for O'Leary, while O'Leary himself received 20 per cent also. Giles was accused of a possible conflict of interest and immediately resigned from the Whitecaps, saying that a full examination of the facts would clear his name. He said he had played no part in the purchase by the Whitecaps of Pierce O'Leary and there was therefore no conflict of interest.

After leaving Vancouver, Giles then took up a long-standing offer to return to West Bromwich Albion, despite all the reservations he had expressed about managing clubs in England. He helped Albion avoid relegation but resigned at the beginning of his second full season in charge, blaming himself for selling too many players as Albion struggled with injuries.

Giles was lured back to the Ireland job, as it didn't involve the huge administrative burden of club management and he would now have the opportunity to work at international level with a much stronger squad of players than he had before. But his professional pride had taken a few severe knocks and he approached O'Neill and Casey with extreme caution. It was the first time Giles had ever applied for a job in his life and he told them that he didn't want to put his name forward only for it to be rejected.

O'Neill and Casey then drove in a rented car to a hotel in Birmingham where they met the Manchester City manager, Billy McNeill, who had an excellent pedigree both as a player and a manager. McNeill had captained the great Celtic team guided by Jock Stein to nine successive Scottish championships and the 1967 European Cup triumph. As a manager he had led Celtic to three championship victories, restoring to the club much of the glory it had lost after Stein's departure. Strife in the boardroom caused McNeill to leave Celtic and he accepted the challenge of rebuilding Manchester City, who had been relegated to the Second Division and who were in penury after the free-spending days of Malcolm Allison. McNeill had helped City win promotion and his team was holding its own in the First Division, but there were limited financial resources available to him. He was anxious to prove himself at international level – the Scotland job was his ultimate prize – and felt he could combine the Irish job with his commitments at Manchester City.

The two FAI officials also contacted the Nottingham Forest chairman, Maurice Rowarth, to see if they could talk to Brian Clough, but were refused permission. They spoke to the Peterborough manager and former Irish international, Noel Cantwell. And in London they met the former Arsenal and Northern Ireland manager, Terry Neill, and the former Irish international, Theo Foley.

Back up north, Casey and O'Neill drove along the M6 in pouring rain and had a furtive meeting in a service station with the former Everton manager, Gordon Lee. Lee was anxious to get back into football but failed to impress.

At the Portland Hotel in Manchester, O'Neill and Casey met the old Manchester United and Scotland player, Pat Crerand. Crerand's parents were from Gweedore in Donegal; Crerand himself had clung to his Irish roots and he was well known for his espousal of the nationalist cause. Crerand would have loved to have played for Ireland. Crerand had done his homework – Liam Tuohy would be his deputy and his team would be built around Paul McGrath – but he was handicapped by his lack of management experience and the FAI's agenda for a new departure.

Also in Manchester, at the Crest Airport Hotel, they interviewed the former Leeds and England centre half, Jack Charlton. Casey had contacted Charlton through the Newcastle United chairman, Russell Cushing. Charlton had walked out of Newcastle and club management a few months previously; he was now spending his time driving up and down the country doing after-dinner speeches and opening businesses; he was in Manchester doing a fishing programme for Channel 4. It was his first break from professional football in more than 30 years and he was enjoying it immensely. Like Giles he had developed a hatred of the growing administrative burden placed on club managers, but his aspirations to manage a national side were well known.

Charlton talked to the two Irishmen for about an hour. He mentioned that he had applied for the England job ten years previously and hadn't even received a reply from the Football Association at Lancaster Gate. He was obviously enthusiastic about the job and made it clear that he would not be going back into club management. He was asked where he would reside if he got the job. Charlton said that the future of the team would lie in England rather than Ireland, as full-time football was vital for international purposes. Since the players were in England, it was natural for him to live in England. Charlton stressed that he knew all the club managers in Britain and would not make a big fuss if he couldn't get the release of players, as he was sure he could get them again. He told them he had never seen Ireland play before but expressed amazement that they hadn't ever qualified for the World Cup or European Championship. They had some very good players – he named Lawrenson, Brady and Stapleton – and he was sure he could get more out of them than the previous manager. It was a blunt interview.

Back in Ireland O'Neill and Casey interviewed a few home-based candidates, the Shamrock Rovers manager, Jim McLaughlin, a former international, Paddy Mulligan and Liam Tuohy, who had the most attractive credentials. Despite the new thinking within the FAI about a British-based manager, Tuohy was emerging as a strong candidate. He had taken the Irish youth team under his wing and they were by far the most successful of any of the Irish international sides, qualifying for three European Championship finals and a World Cup. He had also demonstrated a deft hand at dealing with English club managers. He exploited Giles' Leeds connections, courting the Leeds manager of the time, Eddie Gray. As a result he was able to recruit two English-born Leeds apprentices, Terry Phelan and John Sheridan, into the Irish youth set up. His successes had earned him the support of the representatives of junior football within the FAI and he was also the people's champion. In a survey conducted by the Republic of Ireland Soccer Supporters Club after Hand resigned, Tuohy attracted more than 50 per cent of the votes, while the next contender, Billy McNeill, got only 10 per cent. There was virtually no support for any of the other candidates. 'I think it is highly unlikely that a foreign man will be appointed,' wrote a correspondent in the *Supporters News*. 'With many people not exactly ecstatic with the present squad containing too many English-born players, imagine the outcry if an Englishman became manager.'

It was shaping up to be a tough race and it wasn't long before the first of the runners dropped out. The names of the candidates being considered were officially a secret, but there had been a stream of leaks from the FAI and the selection procedure was the source of an ongoing public debate. Over in Birmingham, Giles had become nervous about negative reaction from the press and public to his candidacy. A few days before Christmas 1985, he rang Des Casey and told him he was withdrawing. 'I know there is some hostility to my style at home,' he said at the time. 'Despite the fact that I wanted the job I didn't want to get involved in controversy. It's a tough enough job without starting off with less than wholehearted support.'

As Giles stepped out, Hand stepped in again. At a meeting on 3 January Des Casey reported that he had received applications from Mark Lawrenson and Eoin Hand, but it was decided not to conduct any more interviews. The FAI now drew up a shortlist for the job: Billy McNeill, Jack Charlton and Liam Tuohy were the names on it. The list was approved by the FAI Council, which then granted the Executive the power to make the final decision. Of the three, McNeill was the man that the FAI wanted. He fulfilled their stated objective of getting a professional British-based manager. Although he had heavy commitments with City, and Charlton was spending his time out shooting game and making after-dinner speeches, McNeill's strong connections with Celtic made him a more politically acceptable choice. As Gerry Callan wrote in the *Sunday Tribune* at the time: 'He [McNeill] is a Celt and would thus have a decided advantage in dealing with the Irish players in comparison to Charlton, who has spent his entire playing and managerial career in the north of England, an area whose people are renowned for their dour and blunt attitudes. Admirable qualities they may be in many ways, but more to the point in relation to the FAI's quest, they are nevertheless alien to the Irish temperament.'

On 9 January Des Casey flew to Manchester to meet the Manchester City chairman, Peter Swales, to see if he could do a deal with him to secure McNeill's services. On behalf of the FAI, Casey offered City financial compensation in return for the release of McNeill on international duty, for between 20 and 30 days a year. At Maine Road, Swales, the directors and McNeill met to consider the offer but turned it down on the basis that it wasn't in City's interests. McNeill's name was withdrawn from the shortlist.

The field was now narrowed down to Charlton and Tuohy, with the Irishman firm favourite. Tuohy's popularity dismayed the faction within the FAI which wanted a British-based manager. A member of the Executive Committee, Fran Fields, rang Giles and asked him to re-enter the race. He said that with McNeill out of the reckoning, the path was now clear for him to get the job and his fear of rejection was unfounded. A number of other members of the Executive also sent him messages of support. Eamon Dunphy went to Birmingham to put pressure on Giles to come back into the race. With the job seemingly within his grasp, Giles rang Des Casey and told him he would like to be reconsidered. He then started making arrangements to come to Dublin to accept again the mantle of Irish football.

But Giles had been misled somewhat. His readmission into the race was being opposed by Tuohy supporters and the FAI Executive split into two bitterly opposed factions. Casey, O'Neill and Fields were in the one which wanted a British-based manager such as Giles. The Honorary Treasurer, Charlie Walsh, led a group in favour of Tuohy, which consisted mainly of junior legislators.

Despite being ideally positioned for the job, Charlton's name hardly figured in all the speculation, except when it came to dismissing his candidacy. 'Although the FAI are maintaining a "front" in contacting Jackie Charlton before making a decision, it is now unlikely that he will get the call,' wrote John Brennan in the *Evening Press*. 'The very fact that he was willing to leave on a sunshine holiday when the Irish manager's post was being decided is hardly indicative of his strong commitment to the idea.'

The search for a manager had now been going on for at least three months but there was still no end in sight. The strain was beginning to show in Merrion Square. An announcement of the new manager was expected at the next meeting of the Executive Committee on 10 January. At the beginning of the meeting, Des Casey as President condemned leaks of the discussions and then asked each member of the Committee individually if he had spoken to the press. Three of them had been having a meal in a hotel when they were joined by journalists, but they said that no information had been given. The meeting broke up again without any agreement on a manager.

'The thing started to get very political,' says Casey. 'Camps started forming within the Council. For instance there was still an ethos there that the concept of a non-national such as Charlton was unacceptable, the media were not at all receptive to it. The media were writing about this every day. There were people who thought with Johnny Giles that the sun shone out of his arse and Liam Tuohy was the greatest thing since sliced pan. But there was also antipathy towards John Giles because of the type of square ball football that he played and the fact that he had been there before and had walked away from it.'

The stalemate over whether the readmission of Giles should be allowed went on for two weeks, with neither side conceding. Eventually a compromise was reached which would mean that Giles, having been asked to rejoin the race, would be sacrificed. A new candidate – the fourth man – had emerged in the 24 hours before the vote took place, and there was furious canvassing of a section of the Executive to rally support for him.

The fateful meeting of the Executive started at eight p.m. on 7 February 1986. All 19 members gathered in the Council room on the ground floor of 80 Merrion Square. The first item on the agenda concerned the draw for the fifth round of the FAI. The Honorary Treasurer then appealed to clubs to send in their cup percentages as there were debts of over IR£30,000.

The next item was the selection of the international team manager. Des Casey reported on his talks with the Manchester City chairman and also on the phone call from John Giles asking that he still be considered for the job. Mr Casey said that as other suitable options were left open by the Council, both he and Dr O'Neill had separately investigated other candidates but he wouldn't put their names forward unless the Committee agreed.

There then followed an hour-long debate on whether to allow Giles back into the race. Several Executive members pointed out that the Council had given the Executive power to elect somebody only from the approved shortlist, which did not have Giles' name on it. But it was Charlie Walsh, a presumed Tuohy supporter and hitherto a stickler for correct procedure, who proposed that new candidates be allowed in. The motion was supported by Tony O'Neill and carried by a clear majority. O'Neill wanted the meeting postponed for a few days as he had again made contact with Brian Clough, who was still interested in coming to some kind of arrangement with his club which would allow him to do the Irish job. But O'Neill's request for more time was rejected by the meeting.

Casey said he could now put forward the name of another new candidate, the former Liverpool manager, Bob Paisley. Casey said he had spoken to Paisley and he was very active in football, and Liverpool, where Paisley was now a director, would have no objections. Paisley was not fussy about a salary but would want to know who his back-up man would be. It had been agreed that this man would be Tuohy, hence the support from the Tuohy faction for the change in procedure which allowed both Giles and then Paisley to enter the race.

It was quite a coup to get Paisley. He was the most successful manager in English soccer history, having won seven League Championships and three European Cups during his ten years as Liverpool manager. But the announcement of his candidacy caused uproar in the chamber. One supporter of Giles, Pat Grace, expressed outrage at what he said was a hidden agenda. He said that Giles had only been reintroduced so that procedures could be changed and Paisley could then join the race also. The Secretary, Liam Rapple, said it was no wonder the organisation received bad press, and he had heard that members were swapping votes for the Vice-Presidency of the Association to have their man elected. Besides the indignation over the manner of Paisley's introduction, there was the argument that Paisley, at the age of 65, was too old to take on the job.

It was the second time that Paisley's name had surfaced in relation to the job. The first was during Hand's tenure when a group on the FAI Executive had approached him about taking over from Hand after Ireland's disastrous start to its last World Cup campaign. He had shown some interest, but Hand supporters had then leaked details of the approach to the press. Paisley was very embarrassed. Des Casey, who had strong connections with Liverpool and was a friend of the club secretary, Peter Robinson, was forced to deny that he had spoken to Paisley.

When Hand resigned, Casey said he approached Liverpool where Paisley had become a director after resigning in 1983, but was told that Paisley wasn't interested. In the weeks running up to the election, that scenario changed. Paisley had been restless outside management and had made comments critical of the new Liverpool manager, Kenny Dalglish. An associate of Casey's contacted Liverpool again and was told that Paisley would let his name go forward. But what Paisley wanted to avoid was any further embarrassment of the type caused when his name was last linked with the job. Like Giles, Paisley would only put his name forward if he was assured of success.

Despite the hostility from some members of the Executive when Paisley's name was suddenly introduced by Casey, that success looked guaranteed. Under the Executive's voting procedure, an absolute majority of ten or more votes was needed to secure victory. As President, Casey would only have a vote in the event of a tie between two candidates. In the first ballot Paisley received nine votes – the others, Charlton, Giles and Tuohy, received three votes each. Paisley was just one short of the figure he needed and was almost home. But the last vote was never to come.

'The rationale behind most of the people on the Executive was genuinely to get the best person,' says Tony O'Neill. 'We wanted a change. I think a lot of people showed a lot of character and a lot of integrity when it came to the crunch. Some members of the Committee resented the fact that Paisley had been brought in at the last minute and they would under no circumstances vote for him. They had picked their person on the basis of what the shortlist had been and they were going to stick with it.'

With Giles, Tuohy and Charlton tying for second place, a second ballot was required to see who should be eliminated first. Tuohy lost out. A further ballot was held – Paisley still had nine votes, Charlton five and Giles four. Giles was eliminated and it was now a straight run off between Paisley and Charlton. Paisley still had a strong advantage, but it was clear that the there was a growing mood of bewilderment and hostility about the surreptitious nature of the introduction of Paisley. It affected even those who voted for Paisley originally. For when the results of the final ballot were announced, it became clear that one of Paisley's supporters had switched his allegiance. Paisley had only eight votes, and Charlton was elected Irish manager with ten. Casey wasn't required to use his casting vote in the end. To this day it's not definite who changed his vote, though Charlie Stuart in the *Irish Press* has named Colonel Tom Ryan, who at the time was *aide de camp* to President Hillery and the Army's representative on the FAI.

The press were waiting outside for the outcome. As the meeting was breaking up, one of the FAI officers, Joe Delaney, was desperately trying to contact Charlton at Cairn Lodge, his home near Newcastle. But the telephone kept ringing out. Then Casey faced the press.

Would Charlton take the job? Casey said he didn't know. The last time he had spoken to Charlton was on 20 January, which was nearly three weeks back. How long would his contract be for? Casey didn't know. The press conference ended without Casey mentioning Paisley's candidacy and how close he was to getting the job.

The former Liverpool manager was waiting at the other end of the phone and Casey contacted him to tell him the bad news. Paisley told him that he was sure Charlton would do a good job. The other manager-in-waiting, Giles, was at the Berkeley Court Hotel about a mile away with some friends. Tim O'Connor, the head of RTE television sport, was there and on news of his appointment was hoping to persuade Giles to go straight over to the studio and on to the live chat show, *The Late Late Show.* Eamon Dunphy came over from Merrion Square and dropped the bombshell about Charlton. More drinks were ordered instead.

With *The Late Late Show* already on air, an assistant handed the host Gay Byrne a piece of paper. Byrne scanned it: 'I've just been handed a piece of paper here which says that Jack

Charlton has been appointed manager of Ireland,' he announced. Putting the paper to one side, he added, 'Whatever that means.' One man in the audience let out a whoop of delight, otherwise there was silence.

Chapter Seven

MY WAY

'I HAVE ALWAYS BEEN the one who took a different direction to what took place under Don Revie at Leeds. I'd looked at different directions, I don't think Gilesy, Billy Bremner or Eddie Gray ever had looked at different directions. I think they were fuckin' committed to a way of playing and a type of game that virtually was a carbon copy of what they knew in their lives before. I've done things differently. And I've suffered for it a lot because people have got this idea that I don't know about football, all I know about is motivation, humping the balls up, chasing fuckin' this. A load of crap. I am the only staff coach that Elland Road has ever produced apart from Freddie Goodwin. I was a staff coach at the age of 26, 27; that's an appointment by the FA by people who look at you and fuckin' know that you know what you're talking about and you've looked into the game a little bit deeper. Now, I never got the Elland Road job, but I tell you something, if I had of got the Elland Road job, I might have left it as it was, if it needed leaving as it was. I might have changed things if I felt it needed change. But I am capable of producing change and I am capable of playing a different design and playing a different pattern and looking at me players and saying, "Where will I get the best out of them?" That's because I've been a student of the game for years, long before Gilesy and Billy and Eddie Gray and Clarkie and all the rest of them. They never did fuck all what I've done. So I feel that I've worked at the business to have the right to produce something different that fuckin' works.

'A manager's job is to make a team out of what they are good at. When you're the boss, you've got to make the fuckin' decisions. I always understood that was standard procedure. Because if nobody ever makes decisions nothing ever gets done. Unless you say to someone, "Do this", not "Ah well, do it occasionally." That's not making a decision, that's hedging a bet. Do it. And I've took the attitude with the Irish all along, "Don't fuckin' argue. Just do what I tell you." So I say to the full backs, "Don't do this. Do that. And if you don't fuckin' do it, you don't fuckin' play. And I say to the centre backs, you do this, if you don't do it, you don't fuckin' play."

'With a national side, you standardise everything. I'm a coach and it's painfully obvious when you take the job that you've got to stabilise and get a pattern of play that everyone recognises. So you get your deadball situations right first. You practise three or four free kicks, not too many to start with, very simple, easy ones to remember, so that you repeat them every time they come in.

'As far as the team pattern is concerned, you must establish a pattern of play and you look at your players and you think, "Well, what have I got?" Now, any manager that doesn't look at his players and then decide what he's gonna play is not doing his job. When you come into a job and you've got a header of the ball like Frank Stapleton – I mean Frank is the best header of the ball that I've ever seen, for his size; bright lad, understands what you ask him to do. There's no use having a great header of the ball unless you can get the ball in to him in certain ways. So the whole business of football is about letting people know what you want and then working towards making the pattern better.

'You start with the goalkeeper. Now, the first thing I said to the goalkeeper is, "You do not, under any circumstances, throw the ball out to one of your full backs. You kick every ball." In other words we're going to start playing from the other end, not from this end. Now, you make it very plain. He might say, "What about . . ." Nah, nah, no. You can't say "Yes" one time and "No" another. The only time is when the full back knows he can get into the opposition half without being tackled. What you say to the goalkeeper is, "I want you to kick every ball long, as high as you can into their half of the park."

'Then you go on to your full backs. What do you want of your full backs? First off, "Forget you're attackers, you fuckin' start off as defenders first. You're a defender. So you've got to close wingers down, you've not got to let them get on the ball if you can help it. When they are on the ball you've got to get close enough, you've got to tackle and you've not got to let 'em get crosses in." And you say to your centre backs: "Centre backs. Centre backs. You've got to pick up and mark, but you can get people back into positions to mark people easier if you tell 'em, and then you pick up the spaces, and you go win the ball, 'cos you're normally the two big lads. You go attack the ball, you go get the bloody thing. Don't be dragged about by somebody who takes you to the near post or takes you to the far post. You pick up the positions to stop people attacking your goal with headers. And you get the ball first."

'And then you talk about your midfield. How do you want your midfield to play? Now, you can't do anything with your midfield until you've really decided on your total team pattern. And I've decided now to play behind the opposition. So where do you start? Well, the logical place to start is with your back four because they get the ball first. I like the full backs to deliver the ball because they play a ball that stays in play down the line. The centre back plays it at an angle that a ball will go out of play on a throw in. So it's better for the centre back to knock it to the full back, for the full back then to look up, see the space behind their full back and knock the ball into it. If he keeps doing that, your forward players very quickly get attuned to know where the ball is going to go. Now, because you're knocking a ball behind people, you've got to push behind it because you know one of your guys is going to get to that ball and he is going to want help, so you push your midfield forward.

'You can't have two midfield runners that go challenging off and running all over the place and leaving midfield bare. Or you can if you do something about it. That means pushing one of your centre backs into midfield which leaves you one on one at the back but then you might push a full back across to cater for that or you might push the full back into midfield. There's all sorts of ways of looking at the game of football and I look at the options I've got and I look at the strengths of the players. I know my strengths, but I also know my fucking laxities.

'Now when you get to the last third of the field it becomes much more difficult because then there are a lot more defensive players picking up areas, picking up spaces. You've got players who can't be programmed, the only thing you can programme is where your big centre forward goes. Because you can always work the ball in a left- or right-sided position and get it to somebody who will have time to throw that ball in at the far post for a big six-foot-four guy to change the direction of the ball, knock it down, get a header on goal or something. But in having a big six-foot-four guy it gives you more options by anchoring him in the midfield; he attracts attention, now you've got more room to play in other areas.

'You can't give players too much information going on to a football field. For the game of football, it washes everything from your mind, all you're doing is concentrating totally on the football, and on the game. You don't have time to think of things. You've got to practise things until they become automatic in your game, they become part of your game, you do them automatically. Now, the two people I ever get doing things automatically first are me full backs. Give 'em the ball, the first thing they do is turn, if they've got room, up the line. Automatically. Don't knock it infield, because your centre forward's already on his way behind the full back. Or your midfield player is already on a run behind the full back. If you start playing balls into midfield you're going to cause confusion because he doesn't know whether you're going to play a long ball or play a ball into midfield. As long as everybody has one thing to do in their game and know what it is, there's no confusion. But once you make it two things to do in the game, now you're causing confusion.

'So all the things that you do in putting a team together, then you refine it over the years. Then you get a bit different here. Then you add a fresh ball into there. Then you add a bit more movement into here. But basically your pattern is established and stays.'

Chapter Eight

BAPTISM OF IRE

JACK CHARLTON was at his hunting lodge at Coverdale in north Yorkshire when the telephone rang. It was an old English journalist friend and team-mate. 'Congratulations,' he said to Charlton. 'If you're not careful you're going to be working again very shortly.'

'Why?' Charlton asked.

'You've got the Irish job.'

Charlton's appointment was initially overshadowed by the belated discovery by the press of Paisley's candidacy and the subsequent recriminations. Paisley's name only emerged publicly a day after the vote had taken place. 'If it is not overstating the case to suggest that the FAI now finds itself with a manager it does not want,' Peter Byrne wrote in the *Irish Times*, '. . . the end product is that a bitterly divided Association now finds itself committed to a manager who was, possibly, even more surprised than they to discover that he had headed the poll on the fifth ballot.' Noel Dunne, in the *Irish*

Independent, spoke of a wedding ceremony he had attended, 'which I am quite sure led to a relationship which will endure far longer than that as yet unconsummated marriage between the bold Jack and the FAI'. Charlton's only supporter in the media was Eamon Dunphy writing in the *Sunday Tribune*. 'Leadership, a sense of purpose, has been restored to Irish football at international level. Decentskinsmanship has finally been dispensed with.'

Four days after his appointment, Charlton came over to Ireland. Like most of his compatriots, he knew little about the country. In the early seventies, he had travelled over with Leeds for a few pre-season friendlies in Dublin. Between games they had gone to a few pubs, to the Carrolls Irish Open golf championships out in Woodbrook and to the Horse Show in Ballsbridge. Charlton had organised to come over on a fishing trip for a week in Kerry with some friends after one of those trips to Dublin, but a strike by post and telecommunications workers meant they couldn't confirm their hotel booking and the holiday was cancelled.

Arriving as manager–elect, Charlton was driven to Merrion Square where, in the basement, he had a meeting about the job with Des Casey and other FAI officers. It's a story that he has added to the repertoire for his after-dinner speeches. He was asked how much he was expecting for the job. Charlton wasn't doing the job for the money; he replied that he was happy with whatever Eoin Hand had been getting. That figure hovered at around IR£15,000 a year. 'When they told me what they were offering me, I told them I wanted a bit fucking more than that. I got a bit more, but not much. But then again, they didn't have any money, the FAI were bankrupt, near enough.'

Charlton then went off to the Phoenix Park races with an FAI official, Joe Delaney. People kept coming up to him and shaking his hand. It was clear that there were no great expectations for the team when one punter told him: 'I hope you get them going a bit faster than those moving statues.'

It had been a good day, both for Charlton and the FAI

officials, who were relieved that their hard-nosed and combustible new manager had been so accommodating on the question of money. But now they were off to meet the press, who were sceptical about the appointment of Charlton and had a bone to pick with Casey. The venue for the press conference was unusually upmarket, the Westbury Hotel just off St Stephen's Green in the centre of town.

The 19 members of the Executive sat at a long table with Charlton in the middle. Charlton quickly charmed the assembled gathering. Anxious not to make the same mistakes as Don Revie, he gave out his home telephone number and told journalists that if he wasn't there he would get back to them. Charlton was asked if he felt uneasy about being the first foreigner to be appointed Irish manager: 'Maybe if an Irishman in England had been appointed you would have considered yourself better off, but as far as I am concerned this is always the type of job that I want to have a go at, and I will give it everything I have to make it a success.

'I am going to do the job to the best of my ability,' he told them. 'And I would like to make one thing very clear. While I do not clock in at this place or that place, I am not a part-time manager, and as well as watching games in England, since your matches are on a Sunday, you'll be seeing quite a lot of me in Dublin and elsewhere.'

The press conference appeared to be winding down gently with the assembled journalists charmed by the Englishman's affable presence, but it was to end with a bang when Peter Byrne of the *Irish Times* said he wanted to ask Des Casey about the Paisley affair. Casey, looking briefly at Charlton, responded that this was the wrong time and the wrong place for such a question. Charlton joined in, saying that it was an embarrassing and irrelevant question. Eamon Dunphy then interjected, saying that it was in the public interest that Casey answer the question.

'Public interest,' Charlton said. 'Public interest. I know you. You're a fuckin' troublemaker, you are. I'm not going to argue with you. I'm bigger than you. If you want to step outside, I'm ready now.' Jack then stood up and grabbed his cap. 'I'm off.' There was a football match on television he wanted to watch. Most of the journalists present saw him off with a round of applause.

★

Charlton's spat with a couple of journalists illustrated his deep distrust of the media, which had built up from years of dealing with an altogether more fearsome strain of the species, the tabloid press in Britain. His next outburst was a more serious one, which is still resounding through the grassroots of Irish football.

Unlike Paisley or Giles, Liam Tuohy, the Irish youth team manager, hadn't been surprised when his application to take charge of the senior side had been rejected. 'The FAI had let it be known that they wanted an English-based manager and I had been happy enough about that,' Tuohy says. 'The reason I put my name in the hat was that if they didn't get the type of manager they wanted from England and they were going to appoint a local person, I was one of the logical people to be involved.' He had also managed to see the funny side of what had unravelled at Merrion Square. 'It was a two-horse race,' he said, 'and I finished fourth.'

As one of the most respected figures on the domestic scene, Tuohy was seen as the ideal figure to act as Charlton's assistant manager. And when Charlton came to Dublin as Irish manager, Tuohy had been asked by an FAI official to meet him at the Westbury. In his hotel room, Charlton said that he hadn't asked to see Tuohy, but they would have a chat anyway. Tuohy filled Charlton in about his job as youth manager. Charlton told him that he hadn't yet decided what he was going to do about his support staff. Tuohy told him of his team's efforts to qualify for the European Youth Championships, and both men agreed that Tuohy would at least see out the last couple of matches.

Three weeks later, the youth team, attempting to qualify for their fourth European Championship found themselves in

Yorkshire on a foggy, freezing day, for a match against England. Charlton arrived unexpectedly at the team's hotel on the day of the match and told them he would be at the game as another one he had been planning to watch had been cancelled because of bad weather. He joined them for lunch, taking issue with the team's selection from the menu.

'We had a chat during lunch, but I felt that he was in a bit of a tetchy humour,' says Tuohy. 'He made observations about the meal – the boys were having steak. I said, well, it hasn't done them too badly because they've reached three European Cups and a World Cup finals. He made this observation about pasta, and about what the new thinking in the game was. So I wondered was he spoiling for something.'

The game at Sheffield was also called off at the last minute, but Elland Road in Leeds was available. They headed off, Charlton in his car and the team on their coach. Before the boys were about to go on the pitch, Charlton dropped into the dressing-room to wish them luck. Tuohy suggested to him that he come back in at half-time if he had any observations to make. Then Charlton took his place in the stand.

Ireland, a small team who played neat football, were 2-0 down at half-time. Charlton didn't like what he saw. It was a freezing cold evening, so cold that the water in the doctor's bucket was turning to ice. But, as the doctor observed, it got very hot in the dressing-room at half-time.

'We didn't have a good first half,' says Tuohy. 'At half-time I always like to sit the players down, give them a cup of tea, make sure everything is alright, then say what you have to say. So they were sat down with their cups of tea, and I stood up to give my party piece. And in comes Jack, walks directly in front of me, not a "by your leave" or "excuse me, Liam". He just ignored me as if I wasn't there. I couldn't believe he had the bad manners to do a thing like that. He was quite forceful in his comments and some of the things he said were very negative. Everything he said was very negative. He wanted the long ball. I was getting midfielders coming back where the ball would be played to their feet. His comments had an edge to them. Mine would have too; you're looking for something from them and you have to be forceful. But he undermined my position in front of the players.'

There were no goals in the second half and Charlton reappeared in the dressing-room when the game was over and delivered another talk. 'In general he talked about the way the game should be played. At that stage I was past listening. I just wanted to get out of the place. If he wanted to say to me, "Get them to do this", that would have been his role. But he shouldn't have come in, and all he was short of doing was knocking me aside.'

When the team got back to Dublin, Tuohy handed in his resignation to the FAI. His assistants, Brian Kerr and Noel O'Reilly, went with him. 'I was in the position that I take the shit he was giving me and stay on – I was doing the job for nothing – I didn't need that,' says Tuohy. 'I mean, I had been a manager of the national senior team. It was not like I was some rookie coming in.'

'Liam Tuohy caused me more aggravation when I took the job on over here than anyone else. I went over to Sheffield because I had just been appointed to the job. And obviously I'm now manager of the Football Association of Ireland. My responsibility is to every team that represents the FAI anywhere.

I went into the dressing-room before the game. Liam said, "Do you want to say anything to them?" I said that I'll have a look at them in the first half and if I see anything that has a bearing on the game, I'll say it at half-time. So I came in at half-time and Liam was doing his talk to them. And Liam said do you want to say anything to them. And I said: "Yeah, a couple of things. Just a few technical things in football." Then they went out and played the second half. They were getting beat 2-0 at half-time and they got beat 2-0. But they were tighter, they were better, they had closed things down, and a few of the things I had said at half-time, I felt they had done better in the second half. I went in after the match. All I said was, "I enjoyed the game. Sorry you lost, these things happen, but when you get the game going right, and we put things right, you'll improve, you'll be better." Then I left. And then all of a sudden – I thought Liam was going to work and keep an eye on things for me – instead of which Liam Tuohy resigned.

'I was left with bloody international sides all over the place, matches coming up. I didn't know anybody in Ireland. I didn't know anybody in the office. I didn't know anybody on the football side over here and I'm left with the whole bloody thing. And Tuohy just dropped me on me head.'

Charlton had a meeting with Brian Kerr and Noel O'Reilly to try to persuade them not to resign along with Tuohy. 'I said: "The least you can do is see if you like me, stay with me for a few months and just see. Don't walk off now, because things might get great here and you might regret it." And they were all muttering something and then I got a phone call to say that they were going with Liam. Hey, Liam made a bloody big mistake. He could have been on the inside and now he's on the outside. Now, with everything that I've achieved, the one thing that gives me great pleasure is that I stuffed it up his arse. That gives me great pleasure. Whatever I've achieved here is with no help from him. And I want people in this country to understand that.'

Charlton's treatment of Tuohy dismayed FAI officials; many of them had hoped that Tuohy would be made the side's Irish-based assistant manager. But there was no open dissent. 'It was not an issue to remonstrate with the manager over what happened to Tuohy,' says Des Casey. 'The priority was to let Charlton have a good shot at it with the senior international team.'

Moreover, the officials were preoccupied with the fall-out from the debacle of 7 February. One member of the Executive, Pat Grace, handed in his resignation at the next meeting. Grace had been a Giles supporter, and he had reportedly placed a bet on him to win. More important, his company, Pat Grace's Famous Fried Chicken, had spent IR£100,000 on sponsorship of the League of Ireland in the previous four years. Grace said that the credibility of the FAI had been seriously damaged and its efforts to raise funds through a forthcoming club lottery would suffer as a result. Grace appeared on RTE in a debate with the Honorary Treasurer, Charlie Walsh. Afterwards, Walsh informed the FAI Council that Grace had said that the people running the Association were capable of fiddling the draw as they fiddled the election of the international team manager. There was outrage over Grace's allegations and he was disqualified from the council.

Charlton was quickly growing accustomed to the workings of the FAI, displaying in the process what was normally a well-hidden facility for flexibility. Initially he had struggled to get the help he needed from the General Secretary, Peadar O'Driscoll, who for nearly 20 years had been the FAI's sole full-time administrator. 'I was not very inclined to go to Peadar for my business, because he didn't do it,' says Charlton. 'I'd give him a list of players for a match and then find that he had added a couple of players to the fuckin' list whom he fancied. I found that the guy I could deal best with was the Commercial Manager, Donie Butler. I would only phone up the FAI between 12 o'clock and two o'clock because I knew that the Secretary would not be in, so that I could ask for Donie Butler and tell Donie what I wanted done and he'd do it. Now, Peadar never argued with me over it, so I think he was quite happy with the arrangement.'

When Charlton took over, O'Driscoll was already over retirement age and he was quickly succeeded by Tony O'Neill. O'Neill was responsible as much as anyone else for the appointment of Charlton, but already he had doubts about the wisdom of the choice. As team doctor, O'Neill had been in the Elland Road dressing-room and witnessed the Charlton outburst. Afterwards, O'Neill had stuck his head over the parapet by complaining at an Executive meeting that Tuohy had been done a grave injustice by the manner of Charlton's visit to the dressing-room.

As General Secretary, O'Neill called Charlton in for a meeting. O'Neill told him that he was unhappy about the arrangement whereby the Commercial Manager was dealing with Charlton's requests. 'Don't phone the office and ask for anything to be done except you do it through me,' O'Neill told Charlton. The manager was unperturbed. 'Tony, I won't,' he replied. 'I'll do everything through you now until I find out that you're not doing what I want you to do. And then if I find that, I will go around in different directions to get things done. But if you do the job the way I want it doing, and the way it suits me, then we'll get on fine.'

The ambitious trips were also out. Louis Kilcoyne approached Charlton about a tour of South America which, Kilcoyne said, would bring IR£50,000 into the FAI coffers. Charlton snorted when he heard that the trip was scheduled for the end of the soccer season, and dismissed the project out of hand. A couple of days later he was talking to the Aston Villa chairman, Doug Ellis. Ellis, in a somewhat bizarre twist, said that the FIFA President, Havelange, was very keen for the Irish trip to go ahead. Charlton gave Ellis a knowing smile; now there would definitely be no trip.

Charlton had put the press in its place. He had put the youth team manager in his place. He had put the FAI in its place. That just left the players.

One of his first moves was to talk to his predecessor: 'I rang Eoin up when I got the job and asked him for a bit of advice about what he did, where he did it, what certain people were like. And I got to know from Eoin about what was going on; who were the players to watch, who were the players to fucking not watch and it's amazing how what he said was almost certainly one hundred per cent right. But you find out yourself, maybe because you've been forewarned about some players, about the Mafia mob that he had with him at the time.

'Some players can be very shrewd – we've got one or two who are very shrewd here at the moment. Particularly when they start getting towards the end of their career and start looking after themselves and they want as much as they can get out of the game. As a last fucking resort. But then when my staff come and start telling me about some of the things they're doing and saying, you say: "Well, that's okay because he'll be out the fucking door within a year. Don't worry, they all get this way. You've got to understand that."'

Charlton's first opportunity to assess how his players performed on the field came when Ireland played Wales, and lost 1-0 in a dreary game in front of only 17,000 at Lansdowne Road. It was shortly after Tuohy had fallen on his own sword and the knives were already out for Charlton himself: 'Jack Charlton talks a great game,' Con Houlihan wrote afterwards in the *Evening Press*. 'Yesterday he produced a stinker. This was the pits, and in a decent country the spectators would be entitled to a refund. And I am tempted to sell my property in Spain and the Canaries and give the proceeds to the FAI. Then they could pay off the manager who never should have been appointed. . . We have the players. The pity is that Brian Clough has so little interest in fishing.'

Charlton himself had his own ideas about who was to blame. He hadn't liked what he saw of one centre half, David O'Leary. O'Leary was one of the three Irish players – Stapleton and Brady being the other two – who for years had been categorised as the world-class players on the Irish team; eventually they would all fall out with Charlton. In O'Leary's case, having been dropped by Arsenal and subsequently by Eoin Hand on a number of occasions, he had already become disaffected with the Irish set-up. Against Wales, O'Leary had a reasonably good game, but his style of standing back from the forward and then using his pace to win the ball was anathema to what Charlton's concept of a stopper should be. He blamed O'Leary for Rush's free header from a corner which won the game for Wales. Charlton hadn't picked the team against Wales;

he had left that to the physiotherapist, Mick Byrne, and he was just there to watch. And as he walked off the pitch Charlton muttered that O'Leary would not play for Ireland again under his charge.

Ireland were going to play in a tournament in Iceland also involving the home country and Czechoslovakia. The tournament was to celebrate the 200th anniversary of the founding of the city of Reykjavik. More attention was being paid to another tournament, the World Cup in Mexico, which was just a week away. Charlton named his squad, and O'Leary's name wasn't on it. It was the first time he had been dropped from the squad in ten years of playing for Ireland, but Charlton didn't inform him before telling the press. His apparent lack of courtesy was to blow up in his face. Like his predecessors, Charlton's plans were being torn up. Ireland's Merseyside contingent, Beglin, Whelan, Lawrenson and Sheedy, decided instead to go off on an end-of-season club holiday. Unabashed, Charlton rang O'Leary for a last-minute call up, but O'Leary had made his own holiday plans and was heading off to Portugal in two days' time.

'I phoned David and said are you coming? And he said, "No, I'm going on holiday." And I said: "Well, it's a bit more important than your holidays, cancel your holiday, you can take them any bloody time." And he said: "Ah no, the arrangements have been made." And I said: "Okay then, forget it." Now, David wasn't to come back to us for three years, but that wasn't my fault.'

As it happened, the Iceland trip was a bit of a holiday. The players arrived laden down with duty-free alcohol, as they had heard there were no pubs in the country. But Charlton also used the gathering to educate the players about how he wanted them to play.

'All I want to give you is a place to start. Now, I want you to do it all the time and I don't want you to deviate from it. What I want you to do is to play the ball so that it gets to our full backs and then the full backs knock the ball in behind their full backs and then I want you all to close 'em up and go chase 'em in their half. Keep knocking the ball and let's see if they can play at the back.'

Ireland won their two games comfortably. 'The Icelanders didn't know what hit them,' Charlton says. 'They never got out of their half. The Czechoslovakians in the next game couldn't get out of their own half. They couldn't understand what was going on. And it caused so much chaos. Just one simple ball played in behind and instead of just one guy chasing it, everybody chasing it.' It was the first tournament the Republic of Ireland had ever won.

The trip also confirmed to Charlton that he had found the centre half he wanted to put his new style into play. Mick McCarthy from Barnsley had joined the squad in the latter days of the Eoin Hand era, and had edged out O'Leary on a couple of occasions, but he had yet to establish himself as a regular first team player. 'I was brought in as a guy who potentially might be good enough to be an international,' says McCarthy. 'I think I was brought in to fill a void for an international trip to Japan when they couldn't get the fuckin' superstars to travel on it, basically. If they had all turned up I wouldn't have got a game. I would still be Mick Who.'

Unlike others who played under Hand, McCarthy's commitment was never questioned, but critics said he would never make it at international level because of his lack of pace. The question of how fast Mick McCarthy could run had led to one of the most shoddy episodes of Hand's tenure. John O'Shea of the *Evening Press* made a bet of £50 with Hand that he could beat McCarthy in a 50 metres sprint. Hand had to convince a reluctant McCarthy to take up the challenge. 'Eoin, in his wisdom, like a prat, said I should race him and I said, "No, I'm not racing him, that's bollocks, that's demeaning me and I'm not having that. Whether I can beat him or not I'm not racing him." And Eoin said, "Nah, nah, that's going to cost me fifty quid if you don't race." Fifty quid was a lot of dosh for me at the time, so I said all right.'

O'Shea, middle-aged, heavily built but intensely combative, was only just beaten by McCarthy. They then had a second race where O'Shea pulled up with an injury. McCarthy himself pulled a muscle in training shortly afterwards – some linked it to his exertions on the running track – and he missed a World Cup qualifying game the following day.

McCarthy and Charlton used to have the odd drink together and talk football in Yorkshire before either was involved with Ireland. By the time the two men found the Irish connection, Charlton was well aware of McCarthy's weaknesses but attached greater importance to his knowledge of the game and the leadership role that his centre half could adopt on the field. 'I've seen better headers of the ball, I've seen quicker people, I've seen more aggressive people,' says Charlton, 'but I haven't seen a bigger and better driver than Mick in pushing the midfield out on to people and making them stay there. And pushing out behind him and dragging people with him and making them come out. In fact Mick fulfilled what I wanted the team to do. Mick fuckin' forced them into it, because it's easy to sit and drop off when instead they should be going forward and competing.'

McCarthy was like a chip off his manager's block. He was a blunt, often foul-mouthed northerner who, if he hadn't been a success on the football field, had a career ahead of him down the mines. He was no Michael Robinson. 'I read what lads say when they come to play for Ireland. Favourite country, Ireland; favourite drink, Guinness; favourite city, Dublin. What are they trying to do? Are they trying to convince people that they are Irish all of a sudden, when they've lived in England all their lives?' says McCarthy.

Mick's father, Charles McCarthy, emigrated from Waterford and settled in Barnsley where he met and married a local Yorkshire woman. Mick used to watch his father practising hurling in fields near the house, but there was little else in McCarthy's life that might have made him identify with Ireland. 'The World Cup in 1966. I was seven years old, living in Barnsley. I wanted England to win. I'd be off my head if I didn't.' Which was how it remained until he was asked to play for Ireland by Eoin Hand. 'I was aware of my Irishness, but it wasn't my country. I wasn't born there, I lived in England all my life, but to get the opportunity to represent me dad in Ireland was brilliant. Half me family is Irish. I've got loads of relatives there. It's not like I'm a distant country bumpkin cousin that's got an aunt and uncle who visited Ireland one time. That's how it's portrayed.'

That's how it might have seemed at the time. McCarthy made his debut against Poland and was tactless enough to admit afterwards that, as he stood for attention for the National Anthems, he couldn't distinguish between the two of them. 'I'd never ever heard the National Anthem, and to be fair, they both sounded similar. I said that jovially as well. It's awful when you look at things in black and white; they look totally different, they're out of context. Somebody was making the point that if you've got an Irish setter, you can play for Ireland. And I said yeah, well, when the National Anthems were played I didn't actually know which was which. My dad didn't go around playing the National Anthem in the house.'

The steady stream of Anglos, as they became known, continued throughout Eoin Hand's period as manager, even though Ireland's results had deteriorated steadily in his last few years. As well as McCarthy, Kevin Sheedy, Tony Cascarino and Tony Galvin made their debuts during this period. When Charlton took over he was quick to exploit this source of talent to the full to strengthen what was becoming an ageing and unbalanced squad. 'I looked at the list of players that were available and I looked at the last Irish team and the first thing that struck me was that you had played six centre backs. And I said: "Ah nah, you can't play six centre backs." They were playing at midfield and full back and centre back. Because namewise they were the best players. Namewise.'

Charlton identified certain weaknesses in the team, up front as usual, and on the right side of midfield. He decided he had to go out and find the talent rather than wait for it to come in, and again he applied a method. 'I circulated the football clubs asking them if they would put a notice on their boards saying that if anyone had an Irish mother or father, or grandmother – going back to grandmother – then I would be interested and I would come and see them.'

Charlton's first port of call was Oxford United, where John Aldridge was creating waves as a striker. Aldridge, after being rejected as a teenager by his home town club, Liverpool, had gone down to Oxford and scored more than 60 goals in three seasons. After an eight-minute hat-trick against Ipswich in November 1985, the Oxford manager, Maurice Evans, felt the time had come for Aldridge to achieve international honours. 'My ideal partnership would be Kerry Dixon with John Aldridge,' he said. 'I think John has the ability to play for his country.'

Aldridge, however, was already 28 years old and still playing for an unfashionable club from which England would not pick its players. 'The fact is,' Aldridge said, 'I'm tired of waiting to see if England will have a look at me.'

Aldridge had been noticed by the veteran Oxford and Ireland right back, Dave Langan. Oxford were a sociable crew – none more so than Langan and Aldridge – and the pair struck up a friendship. During the course of a conversation, Aldridge had casually mentioned his Irish ancestry – his grandmother from Athlone had moved to Liverpool. Langan told the FAI about Aldridge and another Oxford player, the Glasgow-born midfielder Ray Houghton, but they hadn't been brought on board by the time Charlton arrived. After being tipped off again, Charlton acted quickly. 'I went down to Oxford to see a game and approached John in the dressing-room afterwards and I said: "Do you want to play for the Republic? Because you qualify, you know? We've got a few good players there, we need a few more, and we might just mix it a little bit."'

It was a foregone conclusion, but Aldridge had a little surprise for Charlton. He pointed Ray Houghton out to him.

'I had been trying to sign Ray when I was at Sheffield Wednesday and he was at Luton,' says Charlton. 'They said to me that they wouldn't sell him. I didn't know he was at Oxford until John told me. And I said to John, "But he's a Scot. He's a Scottish lad."' Aldridge told Charlton that Houghton's father was from Donegal. 'So I called Ray over, got John to go and fetch him, and I said, "Would you like to play for the Republic?"' Houghton assented, and the three of them stood in the Oxford dressing-room shaking hands.

'So I got two players in exactly the right sort of positions I wanted. Somebody to play up front alongside Frank Stapleton and I've got the right-sided midfielder I need because I had Kevin Sheedy and Tony Galvin on the left.'

When Aldridge and Houghton got called up for the match against Wales, it was the first time that either had been to Dublin. Langan – Dublin-born and reared – accompanied them, like a parent bringing his children to their first day at school. 'They thought there would be problems because of their accent, because Ray is Scottish and John is a Scouser,' says Langan. 'They thought that because there's trouble in Ireland, that English people would get beaten up. Because they had heard of The Troubles in the north they thought that it was in Dublin, because they didn't realise that Dublin was down south and Belfast was in the north.'

The man who helped Jack Charlton in his quest for new talent was Maurice Setters, whom he appointed as his assistant manager. Charlton had ignored calls that he appoint an Irish or Irish-based assistant. He considered it too important an appointment for it to be made for political reasons. Charlton's home is near Newcastle, a terrible place, he says, to do a job from. He had quit the Newcastle job partly because of the amount of travelling involved. There had been one particularly scary incident. 'I was driving along the motorway, coming back from some bloody match in Manchester. I'd driven six hours that day and I was knackered. Suddenly, I realised I was falling asleep at the wheel and I thought, "What am I doing this for?"' When he walked out of Newcastle after being barracked by a section of the supporters, he was, he says, 'only looking for an excuse'.

Setters, a former Manchester United player, had been Charlton's assistant at Sheffield Wednesday and Newcastle. Setters lives near Leeds and within a 60-mile radius of his house there are about 50 soccer grounds. He does a lot of the leg work. 'Maurice loves going to games,' Charlton says. 'He can go to seven or eight games a week and he's still happy.'

As well as chasing up leads about new players, Setters was taking over the Youth and Under-21 teams. His appointment rubbed salt into some wounds at Merrion Square. Charlie Walsh, the Treasurer who had been one of Tuohy's main backers, didn't know whether to be more indignant about the person chosen or the extent of the cost involved. The appointment of Maurice Setters, he complained to Council, was 'a bad joke' and an 'old pals act', which would cost the Association a further ten thousand pounds a year.

Charlton now had a strong squad, and he was determined to get the most out of them. Journalists in Ireland had told him about the problems under Hand of keeping the players under tight discipline. Hand had moved the team headquarters out to the Dublin Airport Hotel, a sensible move since all the players were based in England. Charlton had been irritated to discover that Hertz in Dublin had provided as a perk a fleet of cars at the hotel for the use of the players in the days before a match. 'We used to come over on a Sunday,' says Mick McCarthy, 'and afterwards the Irish lads would just disappear until the game. And there'd be the likes of Chris Hughton, Tony Galvin and me sat in the hotel twiddling our thumbs, not having a great deal to do.'

Charlton was quick to stamp this out and delivered a lecture to the players. 'I just imposed on this squad when they came in the disciplines that were already ingrained at Elland Road that I'd learnt under Revie. That when you go to prepare for the football match, nothing else counts, you're preparing for the football match. What used to happen here, when I first came, was that there were two cars, from Opel or from somebody, that were at the players' disposal. You'd be looking for a player on a Monday or Tuesday afternoon, and you'd be told, "Ah, he's buggered off, he's gone to see his mother and father."

'I had a meeting with the players and I said, "Look, when you come in to play for us, you're here to represent Ireland to play and win an international match and you're here to prepare for two days for that game and we're going to do it properly. You don't go out of the bloody doors of this place without me knowing where you are. You don't blink without you tell me or Maurice. And you get permission from me or Maurice, or Mick Byrne. Because I tell you, it has to be something really important before you're allowed to bloody well go. I want to know where you are. And I've cancelled the cars. And there's none of that any more. While you're here, you're mine."

'And it helped greatly. Because they got so many requests to go to see people who were dying, to see people in hospices, to draw raffle tickets in the school and I took that completely away from them and people, instead of phoning them, would phone me. I'd say, "I'm sorry, but they're here to prepare for a football match and that's it." There was a lot of hassle in the beginning and then people started to accept it and it's been that way ever since.'

The squad – barred from whizzing in separate directions around Dublin – now developed a pattern for their socialising as well as their play. Instead of the Dublin-born players being allowed home in the afternoon, the squad would go into the city centre together for coffee. Then they would go to the movies on Monday night. Even the occasional visit to a pub after the cinema for pints of stout all round is institutionalised. And stays.

'That in itself created team spirit,' says Packie Bonner, who would have had a 400-mile round trip to see his family in Donegal during the pre-Charlton era. 'A far better team spirit.'

The squad were also being won over to the new style of play, even the most skilful among them such as Mark

Lawrenson, who was there for the early part of the Charlton era. 'I've never known such a good atmosphere in a team,' he said later. 'They all play for each other regardless. They have a system which Jack has devised for them which is so simple that they know from one week to the next, one year to the next, that this is the way they are going to play, and they are not dumbfounded or confounded by tactics.'

After the tournament in Iceland, Charlton had gone to Mexico for the World Cup and what he saw only convinced him further that the style of play he was imposing on the team could produce results. 'After two weeks, I hardly made a note,' he says. 'I saw nothing new, just teams playing more or less as they did when I was turning out for England all those years ago. Different names of course. They had got into a rut and I was bored stupid.'

The first big test for Charlton came two months later in Brussels against Belgium, who had just reached the semi-finals of the World Cup. It was the opening match in Ireland's bid to qualify for the European Championships in Germany in 1988. Charlton had insisted that the FAI try to get Ireland's away matches played first. Financially it was a risky strategy, as failure, like in the last World Cup game, would lead to poor attendances at home games. Against Belgium, Ireland came from behind twice to earn a draw in a spirited and well-disciplined performance.

Ireland's next match in the competition – a home game against Scotland – was dominated by the pitch. It appeared that the owners of the ground, the Irish Rugby Football Union, had been expecting the likes of Hastings and Lenihan rather than Hansen and Brady. The grass was so long that the players boots couldn't be seen when they stood still. Since Ireland started playing at Lansdowne Road the pitch had been regarded as a nuisance and an obstacle to producing good football. The IRFU received 15 per cent of gate receipts from international soccer games but refused to cut the grass to the length required by the game of soccer for most of the year as its first commitment was to rugby. It appeared now that Charlton regarded the long grass and uneven surface as a virtue and had given it his tacit approval. After a later game against Spain which Ireland won, the manager of the ground, Tom Kavanagh, said Charlton had thanked him for the state of the playing surface and said that he didn't think the victory would have been achieved without it.

The game against Scotland finished in a goalless draw, with both sides punting the ball at each other over long distances and creating few goalscoring opportunities. It was a dismal offering for the 50,000 supporters at the game and afterwards Charlton faced a gathering of the press disturbed at what they had seen. 'Things take time,' he said. 'The players are still trying to adapt to my way of playing. They are used to doing certain things for their clubs. Now I'm asking them to try something new. It takes more than a couple of games.'

The veteran soccer reporter, Bill Kelly of the *Sunday Press*, put it to Charlton that players should be able to think for themselves. Charlton stared at him, picked up his cap and walked out with the parting words, 'Half of you don't know what I'm talking about anyway.'

Charlton walked out of the press conference, but the away game in Scotland four months later would scatter his critics beyond the horizon. Howls of protest had greeted the line up with centre half, Paul McGrath, at right back and midfielder, Ronnie Whelan, playing in the left back position for the first time in his senior career. Ray Houghton was making his eighth appearance for Ireland, watched by about 20 of his relatives, all of whom, with the exception of his father James, were rooting for Scotland. Lawrenson, moved into midfield, scored from a quickly taken free kick after seven minutes and the Irish – with Houghton outstanding – never allowed the Scots back in the game. Many local supporters of Glasgow Celtic joined several thousand Irish fans, the team and the manager, for a long night of celebrations. It was Ireland's best result since that other European qualifying game in Czechoslovakia in 1967, and this time the rewards would amount to a lot more than a bottle of wine.

At home, the public at large remained generally unmoved by the team's sharply improved performance. Only 17,000 people turned up to see Ireland beat Brazil 1-0 in a friendly game at Lansdowne Road. That victory was further evidence that this team could beat anyone in the world. But in the European Championship, Ireland stumbled, losing to Bulgaria away and drawing at home to Belgium. Ireland then beat Bulgaria 2-0 at Lansdowne Road, but the result appeared to be only a consolation prize for their efforts in qualifying. Bulgaria only needed a point in Sofia against an impoverished Scots side which was fourth in the qualifying group. Three minutes from the end of that game Steve Clark played the ball to Gary Mackay, who had come on as a substitute at half-time for his first cap. On the edge of the penalty box, Mackay smacked it with his left foot into the corner of the net. It was the most important goal ever scored for Ireland. The FAI sent a crate of champagne over to the Scottish FA as a gesture of appreciation. As though they had been sent a hot potato, the SFA sent it back to Dublin, where a big, long party was about to begin.

It began in earnest after Houghton scored five minutes into Ireland's first match in the European Championships against England. Ireland didn't play particularly well that day, but held out due to some poor England finishing and an inspired display by Packie Bonner in goal. Ireland's best display in the Championships came in the next game against the eventual finalists, the Soviet Union. A goal – the most spectacular in Charlton's era – bicycle-kicked by Ronnie Whelan off a long throw in by Mick McCarthy, gave Ireland the lead. They missed several other excellent opportunities and allowed the Soviets to equalise midway through the second half with one of their rare attacks on the Irish goal. Ireland needed a draw against Holland, the eventual winners of the tournament, in their final match in the group to qualify, but they were forced on the defensive for virtually the entire game and Kieft scored for the Dutch nine minutes before the end.

Hardly had the European Championships passed when Ireland began the qualifying campaign for Italia '90. Ireland's problem had always been scoring, and they had failed to get a goal in their first three games against Northern Ireland, Spain and Hungary. Charlton had made a virtue out of speaking openly about his players to the press, and he implied in a television interview that his strikers Aldridge and Cascarino were to blame. In reply, Aldridge pointed out that under the system employed by Charlton, goalscoring opportunities were few and much of their work was taken up chasing the ball in areas where there were no goalscoring opportunities. Aldridge complained that his legs would be 'worn down to stumps' by the time Charlton had finished with him. Aldridge, in contrast to his club form with Oxford and now Liverpool, had scored only once in 23 games for Ireland, but he was still very much part of Charlton's plans.

Charlton was, however, questioning the fitness of Brady and Stapleton to remain on the team. He agonised over how he could drop them and their drawn-out removal from the international stage created intense bitterness on both sides. Charlton didn't have a problem dropping players from the side, except when it came to big names. When Dave Langan was left out of the squad to go to the European Championships it caused little surprise generally but was deeply hurtful for a player whose commitment to Ireland had stood out over an international career lasting nearly ten years. Langan had to read in the newspapers about the end of his international career. 'I didn't go back to Dublin for three years after Jack dropped me. I didn't want to read the papers about "Jack this" and "Jack that". Jack told me afterwards that he should have rang me, but he didn't have my phone number. It upset me mother terrible and I can't forgive him for that. The price of a phone call. All those years you play and then you're not in the team without any explanation. He thanked me for not going to the papers but I did later on.'

Charlton publicly rejected that criticism when it came along. 'I am not an insensitive person and I am aware of the thoughts which go through players' minds when they are coming to that stage of their careers when a parting of the ways is inevitable. It is true that I don't write letters to people or call them on the phone to tell them they are finished. That for me has a ring of finality about it, it smacks too much of a death sentence. I prefer to say nothing and let a player fade out with dignity. I don't particularly want to be the one to tell them officially that they are finished in an Ireland context – with so few players to draw from, that could, in any event, be premature.'

Langan was a terrace hero for his flailing sorties down the right wing, but Brady was obviously a more substantial figure who posed a problem which gnawed at Charlton. 'You have a national hero called Liam Brady who, in my opinion, is one of the best players I ever saw,' says Charlton. 'Great player, Liam. But he wanted to play from the back, in the way that Gilesy's régime and Eoin Hand's régime had done. Liam was taking the ball in his own half from the centre backs. And I cut that out completely. And I said to Liam if you want to play for me you don't get the ball off the back four, get it off the front people. Because I think your ability is wasted while you're farting around in front of your own back four. And it took a while for Liam to get a hold of it and for Liam to understand what I actually wanted and for Liam, I think fairly grudgingly, to actually accept that there might be something in what I was telling him to do.'

'You couldn't be over elaborate when you had the ball,' says Brady. 'Having said that, there's no one going to stop me picking a pass out when I see one. There's no one going to stop Mark Lawrenson or Ronnie Whelan from doing the same. It's when you maybe risk a pass and lose it, that's when Jack blows his top.' When Brady did get Charlton's message, his performances justified his reputation as one of the best midfielders in Europe. He played in all eight of Ireland's qualifying matches for the European Championships, often disobeying Charlton's orders, though revelling in his clearly defined role within the structure of the team. He was fired up at home to Bulgaria and had a superb game, though ten minutes from the end he lashed out with his arm at Sadkov, who had been fouling him repeatedly. The referee sent him off – he had already been booked in the first half – and Brady received a four-match suspension covering the period of the European finals in Germany. This was subsequently reduced to two matches on appeal, but he missed all the games anyway because of a knee injury.

By the time of the qualifying rounds for Italia '90, Brady's level of performance was dipping. He had moved back to Britain and was playing for West Ham, but was debilitated by a number of injuries. Charlton had dropped Brady or taken him off early to blood a new member of the Irish squad, the Norwich City midfielder, Andy Townsend. Townsend wasn't a particularly aggressive player – few on the Norwich side were – but he was energetic, enthusiastic, not short on skill, and he showed a willingness to adapt to Charlton's style. 'Andy sticks the boot in, and the Europeans don't like that,' Charlton said.

As Ireland made an unspectacular start to the campaign for Italia '90 there were calls for Brady to again be given a central role. Charlton found the criticism irksome: 'What Brady can't do at 33 is give me 90 minutes of football at a pace and work rate our style demands,' he said. Brady, normally loath to make comments to the press, snapped back: 'I don't like stupid quotes like that,' he said. 'I take exception to those remarks.' Charlton carefully chose his moment to strike against Brady. Ireland's position in the World Cup qualifying group had been turned round by three home wins in a three-month period over Spain, Malta and Hungary. A friendly game against Germany was now being seen as a match against a possible future World Cup opponent in Rome. Charlton announced a surprise line-up, with Brady, Stapleton and Tony Galvin starting the game. 'With Ireland, you see, they don't give up their fuckin' heroes easily, so you've really got to show 'em. If I don't pick Liam to play or I don't pick Kevin Moran to play or I don't pick somebody that's Irish and been there a long time, they want to know why you didn't fucking pick him to play. And you say, "Well, he's too old, he's not fast enough now. I want somebody who can do better for us in the years to come and I've got to reshape the side." So what I did was I put 'em on display. I had three of them – Liam, Frank and Tony Galvin – who were coming to the end of their time and I put 'em on display to the public.'

Charlton's public display didn't go exactly to plan, as Stapleton scored after ten minutes to put Ireland in the lead and was having an excellent game. His goal shook up the Germans, and they began dominating the game. 'Jack was totally absorbed in the game,' said one of his coaching staff, Noel King, 'and he was becoming more and more frustrated. He was roaring at Liam to pick players up. And then he turned around and said, "Right, that's it."'

'We were getting run to death across midfield,' Charlton says. 'And it was obvious that Liam had had his day. He wasn't tackling anybody. He wasn't getting away from anybody like he used to.'

The Germans equalised after half an hour and three minutes later Brady was replaced by Andy Townsend. At half-time, Brady remonstrated with Charlton in the dressing-room, telling him that he had been humiliated by being replaced so early and it could have waited till half-time. The match finished 1-1. In the hotel afterwards, Brady announced his retirement from international football.

Charlton's plan had worked, even if the execution had been messy, with lots of blood on the carpet, but Charlton denies he deliberately wanted to strip Brady of his dignity. 'Hey, I didn't do it to embarrass Liam, If I thought I was embarrassing Liam I would have left him on. I am a fuckin' pro at the business. That's my job, to get results for Ireland. I'm not going to give up a result against the West Germans for Liam or anybody. I could never give Liam another game. He was a national hero. In my opinion he was gone, he had had a bad leg for a long time, he just wasn't the fuckin' Liam we knew and loved. They would expect me to call him up for every international match in spite of the fact that he's not quick and not playing, so I put him on display. And then after that Liam disappeared off the scene.'

Charlton brought Stapleton to the World Cup, and bitterly scolds himself for doing so. After the game against West Germany, Stapleton was left on the bench for the qualifying game against Northern Ireland at Lansdowne when qualification for the World Cup was virtually assured with a 3-0 victory. Stapleton was then left out of the squad altogether for a game against the Soviet Union. 'I couldn't understand the reasoning for it,' says Stapleton. 'If you go back to the German match, I played in that game and I knew I played well and then I didn't get another chance. I was in every single squad except the Russian one after that, and on the bench every single time thinking to myself, thinking that if he's not going to use me here, he's not going to use me ever. He never came and said: "Look, I'm going to take you to the World Cup, but you're not in my plans, you're not in my 16 to play." He didn't come and tell me. If it was a young player he'd brought in two days before, he maybe could feel he didn't have to tell me why. But I'd been playing 14 years of internationals and I felt I deserved a little bit more than that.'

The subject of Stapleton is one that brings a deep well of bitterness within Charlton to the surface; a froth of emotion which most other men would suppress when at the centre of such a happy story. 'Frank is critical of everybody,' says Charlton. 'You can never do anything right for Frank. Instead of Frank thanking me for stretching out his career and making something of it, he fuckin' always burns his boat, Frank. He's a begrudger.'

After qualification, Ireland went to Malta to acclimatise for a week before going to Italy. Stapleton did get another run out for Ireland when he came on as a substitute in a friendly match against Malta and scored a record-breaking 19th goal. But they were worrying times for Charlton. A number of players – Houghton, McGrath and Whelan – were struggling with injuries. Charlton decided to adjust his squad and called in Alan McGloughlin of Swindon Town, an attacking midfielder, as cover for Houghton. It meant he now had to drop a player from the existing panel. He chose Gary Waddock, who after a number of serious injuries had just forced his way back into the squad. Charlton now believes he made the wrong choice. 'I should have kept Gary because Gary was a smashing lad and he wanted to play. I left him out to take Frank, 'cos I wanted Frank to finish on a high note, but he knew he wasn't going to play because I told him he wasn't going to fuckin' play. He was past his best as well. I've got Niall and Cassy and David Kelly, I don't need Frank, but I took him. Biggest fuckin' mistake I ever made. I should have sent him home in Malta 'cos he was a miserable . . . He didn't help for one minute, he never stopped moaning and grousing. Knowing he wasn't going to fuckin' play, he could have helped and joined in with the training, instead of which he carried on like a spoilt kid.'

Charlton had laid down a few rules for the trip in Italy. He warned the players about speaking to the British press. And he told them that they weren't allowed see their wives or go for walks outside the hotel without getting the permission of the management. Stapleton was derisive. As he later wrote in his book, *Frankly Speaking*, 'To the majority of the players it was like being in school again and we were being treated like children. There had never been any problems with the players in Jack's time as manager, and our attitude had always been first class. We really couldn't believe what we were hearing.'

In Italy, Stapleton and John Byrne, who was used to being on the periphery of the squad, strayed outside the rules. Bored after a week of inactivity, they left the hotel in Sicily and took a boat ride. Charlton found out and confronted them at the quay on their return. 'They knew the rule was that you wear your hats in the sun, they knew the rules that you don't leave the hotel without permission, they knew all of it. And then both Frank and John fucked off in a boat. And I knew it wasn't John's fault. No hats on, no fuck all. And I wanted to know why. And then I should have said to Frank "get your fuckin' passport and fuck off home." But I didn't. I went along with him again. Knowing that it would just cause aggravation in Ireland and I'm better just dropping him and leaving him out. Now Frank had good years with me and I appreciate those years. But I won't treat with silly spoilt children. We've always welcomed Frank, I don't bear grudges, but I could have done with Frank.'

Chapter Nine

Playing Hard Ball

THE RELATIONSHIP between Stapleton and Charlton had also been soured by a dispute over a seemingly abstract question: Who owned the Irish soccer team?

With the success of the team, the question had taken on a compelling supplementary. Was it the FAI, the sponsors, the players or even the manager himself? At stake were millions of pounds worth of profits derived largely from the team's success, and sharp business minds from within the ranks of the players and the FAI were involved in tough negotiations for the spoils.

In 1986, when the Association had borrowed one hundred thousand pounds to tide itself over, it appointed two people who would lead them out of the financial crisis. One was Jack Charlton. The other, not quite so charismatic, though more deliberate, was a Commercial Manager, Donie Butler, previously a business executive with a provincial newspaper. He would head a new commercial division which the FAI had toyed with creating for years. While Charlton initially floundered in a foreign country, Butler, armed with an enormous contacts book, was an instant success. Within a month of his appointment, Opel in Ireland, with the blessing of its parent company General Motors, signed a four-year sponsorship deal for the Irish team, worth IR£400,000 to the FAI. Shortly afterwards, the FAI ditched O'Neills, the Irish company that had supplied the team's kit for more than ten years. O'Neills couldn't come near to matching a deal the FAI struck with Adidas, whereby the German company paid IR£100,000 again over four years, for the exclusive right to provide the kit.

The deals shored up the FAI's desperate financial position. And after Charlton guided the team into the European Championships, the money started to roll in. As Donie Butler said afterwards, 'Many companies, when they saw how the team played in Germany and how wonderfully the Irish fans behaved and the television and news coverage they received, realised what an opportunity they had missed. When 250,000 people turned out to welcome the team home that also brought the message home to them.'

In the run up to World Cup qualification, the bandwagon gathered pace and the FAI raised about one quarter of a million pounds in sponsorship money. All the home games for the qualifying games were full houses, each bringing in gate receipts of IR£400,000 net profit. By 1989 the FAI was able to report a profit for that year alone of nearly IR£700,000. In addition they could look forward to about one and a half million pounds from revenue generated from participating in Italia '90. Much of the money was spent on the badly needed refurbishment and modernisation of the offices in Merrion Square. And, whereas previously the FAI hadn't been in a position to put money into the development of the game in Ireland, nearly two million pounds had been distributed among clubs in improvement grants since Charlton had taken over.

For the European Championships, the Irish squad formed a players' pool, based on a model already used by the English and German teams for big competitions. All fees from the FAI were paid into the pool and then divided among members of the squad. Commercial earnings were extended to all the players who had played in the qualifying games. The players felt they had been badly rewarded for their success in the European Championships. Between sponsorship and bonus payments, the squad received about IR£140,000, about IR£6,000 each, and were amongst the lowest paid in the championship. As Italia '90 beckoned, they decided to flex their muscles and wrestle for themselves a substantial portion of the takings.

The team appointed a four-man committee to represent them in their financial dealings with the FAI and potential sponsors. It consisted of Stapleton, Moran, Brady and Houghton. The first three had a useful pedigree for the tough negotiations ahead. At Arsenal – notably parsimonious employers – Stapleton had bargained to close the gap between his £56 a week wages and the £750 earned by his striking partner, Malcolm MacDonald. The Arsenal manager of the time, Terry Neill, refused to budge until Stapleton complained to the *Sunday People* newspaper about how much he was earning and then put in a transfer request.

Kevin Moran had studied commerce at University College Dublin and had worked for an accountancy firm in Dublin before going to Manchester United. Brady was already a millionaire. One of his mentors, John Giles, had introduced him to the Leeds solicitor, Ronnie Teeman, who had Giles and a number of other sportsmen as his clients. With Teeman's guidance, Brady had moved from Arsenal to Juventus at the age of 24, and had honed his negotiating skills during transfer dealings with men like Gianni Agnelli, the boss of Juventus and Fiat.

The previous managers, Giles and Hand, had carried out negotiations on the players' behalf with the FAI. The sums they agreed on were small and would always remain hypothetical, as Ireland never qualified for any of the competitions. Charlton had told the players that he wanted no part in their financial affairs. But he also said that they should not carry out any negotiations with the FAI, or work on any sponsorship deals, until they had qualified for Italia '90. He did not want the public spectacle of the team negotiating for a competition it had yet to qualify for and he also told the players they would have more bargaining power if they waited till they had actually reached the finals.

The team was however growing increasingly frustrated as the qualifying rounds went on, in particular with the FAI's main sponsor, General Motors. As part of the sponsorship deal with the FAI, GM erected a marquee at Lansdowne Road, where it could entertain guests before and after a game. The players were expected to go to the tent after games and mingle with the guests. When the team were in Dublin for the qualifying game against Spain in April 1989, they held a meeting in the function room at the Dublin Airport Hotel and agreed unanimously that they wouldn't attend the function as Opel had refused to make a contribution to the players' pool. After the game the guests gathered expectantly. But in the dressing-room, Stapleton, in front of the rest of the players, told Charlton of their decision not to attend the Opel function. Charlton was aghast. 'He was at pains to tell us he didn't have a contract with Opel,' says Stapleton, 'yet he was on every advertising board there was in the country. He was at pains to tell us that he had no tie in, but he still at the same time didn't like it. So it was a bit of a conflict for him because he may have said, "Yeah, they'll be in there." We had no deal with anybody, and we felt we were being exploited.'

The players went straight on to their bus and back to the hotel. Later, there was a scene when Charlton approached Stapleton in the crowded foyer of the hotel. In front of astonished onlookers, Charlton gave his hapless striker a verbal lashing. 'He'd had a few drinks after the game,' says Stapleton. 'Jack felt there was a big influence by myself, Liam Brady and David O'Leary on the rest of the squad and I told him that was a load of nonsense. I think he had a bit of a phobia about established players who had been with the team for a lot of

McGrath savours the moment of triumph after the final whistle at Windsor Park
(Tom Burke, Irish Independent)

Dublin's busiest thoroughfare, O'Conell Street, during the Ireland v Italy game
(Sunday Independent)

Charlton congratulates the goalscorer Lawrenson after the landmark victory in the European Championships against Scotland at Hampden (Colorsport)

After four weeks under the Orlando sun, Staunton wouldn't even take his cap off for the national anthem (Sunday Independent)

Houghton, as always on his toes, fends off Maldini and Baresi with Irwin in the background (Sunday Independent)

Charlton comes out of his box to water a wilting Staunton
(Sunday Independent)

EAMON DUNPHY

Give Liam a ring, Jack

Jack Charlton's decision to substitute Liam Brady 10 minutes before half-time on Wednesday was entirely consistent with both his personality and the football philosophy that has placed Ireland among the world's leading soccer nations.

The substitution was insensitive, but Jack has never cared much about people's feelings. He doesn't care about the feelings of players, journalists, or the men in Merrion Square with whom he has minimum contact. What matters to Jack is getting the job done and at the moment he took Liam off on Wednesday the job wasn't being done the way he likes it to be.

Charlton is a complex character, simple in his convictions but not easily explained to anyone outside the cloistered world of professional soccer. For one thing he is, despite his insensitivity to others, extremely sensitive himself. For another he is, unlike most hard men . . . emotional . . . something he doesn't like to show in public or in private.

His first competitive match in charge of the Irish team ended happily, a 2-2 draw against Belgium in Brussels, a result that saw us on our way to West Germany. It was, ironically, Liam Brady's last-minute penalty, converted with splendid courage, which gained us that precious point. Afterwards in the hotel bar a few of us, players, officials and journalists had a sing-song. Jack's contribution was a deeply personal, poignantly emotional song evoking the memory of his father who was a coalminer. "If any of you write about this

Thus the mystery of John Aldridge's failure to score for Ireland as he does for Liverpool, Paul McGrath's playing in midfield instead of centre-half, Ronnie Whelan playing left-back in several of our most important games — notably the victory at Hampden Park over Scotland — and, when he was still fit, the best central defender in Europe, Mark Lawrenson playing in midfield from which unusual position he scored the winning goal in Scotland.

All were willing to leave their club identities behind, all were willing to see things Jack's way. In John Ald-

is pitched 40 or 50 yards from your own goal. Defenders are the principal beneficiaries; when their team has the ball they can stroll forward looking good as they select their passes at will. When they have to defend they do so in numbers, their ranks reinforced by midfield and often striking colleagues.

Ireland's success in international football since Jack took charge has a lot to do with breaking the hearts of opposing defenders and midfield players. We challenge the norm, dictate the rhythm of their game by ensuring that battle is joined in their

flowing the other way, in favour of the blunt instrument, but England still expects its national team to play the Continental game.

Alf Ramsey won the World Cup for England because he properly identified their strengths and others' weaknesses. Charlton has been successful with the Irish team for precisely the same reason. The similarities between Ramsey and Charlton don't end there. Ramsey despised journalists — was openly contemptuous of critics who didn't know what they were talking about. Jack shares that healthy prejudice

fessed afterwards that he had never felt the same about football after the '66 World Cup.

The Liam Brady business this week is somewhat reminiscent of the Greaves affair in '66. Much shock and horror has been expressed. Too much. Charlton's original decision to substitute Liam was crass stupidity, compounded by comments he made afterwards — and indeed things previously said — about Brady's inability to contribute very much to Ireland now and in the year ahead.

Reflecting on this unhappy week we are faced with another facet of

That was unreasonable. Especially so because the Germans are a useful side, who packed midfield, where they were always going to have an extra man for Brady and his Irish colleagues to confront. It was the extra man who scored the German goal . . . that was Jack's fault, not Liam Brady's.

And that's the truth Jack, and I know what I'm talking about. I have 17 years as a professional player, 23 international caps and a pass from your beloved Lilleshall School of Coaching with one of the highest marks ever awarded to prove it.

● PARTING OF THE WAYS . . . Charlton watches a dejected Brady walk out of international football.

Charlton shows Liam Brady the door after 35 minutes of play against West Germany, ending his international career

Campos of Mexico watches Townsend's near-post header narrowly miss his goal
(Sunday Independent)

After weeks of minor skirmishes, Charlton goes toe to toe with FIFA during the Mexico game to earn his £10,000 fine (Sunday Independent)

*His Master's Voice: Charlton, banished to the ITV commentary position, gets his
message across to his assistant, Maurice Setters (Sunday Independent)*

Bonner's joy after the Norway game is shortlived, as he rues his blunder against the Dutch

years. I don't know who fed him that information.' Ray Houghton joined the fray, confirming to Charlton that it had been a decision taken by all the team. Charlton turned on Houghton and lambasted him also. The team captain, Mick McCarthy, was watching the scene from the restaurant, where he was seated with Stapleton's wife, Chris. McCarthy remained rooted to his seat and declined to intervene, contributing to Stapleton's glum mood when they roomed together during the World Cup.

The action by the players rattled Opel as well as Charlton. Later the FAI, acting on Opel's behalf, agreed to pay IR£20,000 into the pool. However, the players agreed that the episode could have been handled better both by themselves and Charlton. 'Frank got picked on afterwards by the FAI and by Jack because Jack as team manager was expected to sort the team out,' says Niall Quinn. 'Unfortunately we should have told him in a room together, but Frank went to tell him on his own.'

The players and the sponsors were soon on collision course again, and this time the courts would have to sort out the problem. The players had adhered to Charlton's demand that they refrain from commercial activities until qualification. However, their agent, Fintan Drury – a former RTE journalist and semi-professional footballer – had already set up deals with a number of major companies who were on the starting blocks. One of them, the building society, Irish Permanent, couldn't even wait for the final whistle in the match against Northern Ireland where a victory for the Republic would virtually guarantee qualification. When Tony Cascarino made it 2-0 for the Republic two minutes after half-time, the commercial director of Irish Permanent took out his mobile telephone. He ordered two vans carrying full-size billboards of the Irish squad wearing Irish Permanent T-shirts to start touring the streets.

Within two days, Opel GM had issued injunctions against both Irish Permanent and Drury Communications to try to stop the campaign. Opel said that it had exclusive rights to the team as sponsors of the FAI. Drury Communications said Opel had no contract with the players themselves and furthermore claimed that Opel was suing Drury rather than individual players because it did not want the rift between sponsors and players to become apparent. The players remained in solidarity with their agent. Frank Stapleton, in a written statement, told the court: 'To the players, it appeared that the main beneficiaries of the success of the team were General Motors and the Association, rather than the players.'

After a brief hearing, Opel backed down, and besides some minor restrictions, the players were given licence to exploit the commercial market. It meant they could greatly enhance their earnings, but it also established an important point of principle. 'Opel felt that since they had a contract with the FAI they owned the Irish team,' says Niall Quinn. 'It was an important thing because it was subsequently proved that they owned us when we were playing for Ireland, but couldn't control what we did with our spare time.'

Opel itself was one of the first companies to come in with a sponsorship offer for the players themselves, and by the time the World Cup approached, half a million pounds had been added to the players' pool from commercial activities.

The confrontation between Opel and the players had a disconcerting effect on Charlton. He had been powerless to stop the players from boycotting the Opel function after the Spain game. Charlton later revealed that when he heard that the players were planning a further boycott of the Opel-sponsored Player of the Year awards – an action which would have been the cause of deep embarrassment – he decided that he would have to resign. The settlement between Opel and the players removed this threat, but Charlton was still under the impression until two days before the Player of the Year event that the boycott was going ahead. Charlton, who thought he had left all the troubles about money behind him when he left club management, described it as the most uncomfortable experience as Irish manager.

After the scrap with Opel, the players went straight into battle with the FAI itself. 'We said we were going to play hard ball,' says Stapleton. 'It's a situation where there's no guarantee for the future and we have to go and get the best deal we could.' At first, it appeared that their decision to hold off on the negotiations till after qualification had back-fired. The players sought a bonus of one thousand pounds per man for each match in the qualifying campaign and also demanded extra payment for friendlies. The FAI, however, refused to negotiate retrospectively. The players were also looking for a figure of approximately IR£700,000 between them from the FAI for the World Cup campaign itself.

The FAI had predicted, correctly, that the negotiations would provide a watershed for their future dealings with the players. At a meeting of the FAI Council, Des Casey warned that if the players were looking for too much money it would create a dangerous precedent which would be likely to rebound on the FAI. The Honorary Treasurer, Charlie Walsh, said that the Association should be aware that in the European Championships of 1988, the Dutch FA gave their players more money than they actually took from the Championships themselves. Liam Rapple said the committee responsible for the development of the game had found that there were huge demands from the infrastructure of the game for the Association's money.

The negotiations went on for several weeks, and days before the team were due to leave for Italy, the players' representatives arrived in Dublin in a tetchy mood for a final round of negotiations with FAI officials. 'We are simply disgusted by the attitude of the Association,' Frank Stapleton said, 'and unless they rethink their approach there are going to be lots of disgruntled Irish players in Italy. There is, of course, no question of the players refusing to give their all in the finals. As usual they will run until they are ready to drop, but this unfortunate business must affect their morale.'

To increase the pressure on the FAI, the players resorted to similar tactics to their predecessors who were then trying to get rid of the Big Five selection committee 20 years earlier. They issued this written statement to the public, this time through their agent, Drury Communications: 'It is deeply disappointing that the players who brought Ireland to their first ever World Cup finals should find themselves in the embarrassing situation of issuing a statement on bonus payments just two days prior to their departure for Italy. That we do so is totally the fault of the Association.

'Negotiations on this issue began months ago. Some weeks ago, we informed the Association that we were totally unhappy with the conduct of the negotiations and pressed for an urgent change in the approach in order to achieve a settlement.

'Lest the notion that we are making excessive demands gain any credence, we are issuing this statement on behalf of all 22 players in the squad for Italy.

'The players were initially told that the FAI would not, and could not, negotiate retrospectively. We pointed out that the manager had instructed the players that negotiations were not to begin until qualification was secured. We followed that instruction and now we are being penalised.

'The players are demanding match fees of one thousand pounds per game, retrospectively for the matches played since the European Championship ended. This is the major sticking point between us, so it is worth clarifying the players' position.

'For all the home qualification matches, each player received a match fee of IR£250. The four World Cup qualifiers are known to have netted the FAI a minimum of IR£1.5 million.

'For all the recent home friendly international matches – with gate receipts up as a result of the increase in ticket prices – the FAI comfortably netted a further one million pounds. Our take was IR£150 per player, or IR£9,000 in total for the three matches.

'They have succeeded admirably. We are in a difficult position and we are bitterly disappointed to find that we now have to negotiate in public. To those who might suggest that we are being greedy, we ask them to look again at the figures, and far more importantly to those who might question our determination to compete in Italy, they need have no fears.

'This matter could easily have been resolved months ago. We did everything possible to ensure it was.'

The public response was overwhelmingly in favour of the players; one newspaper poll found that 85 per cent of people supported their stance. Even though the players never threatened any sort of overt protest, the prospect of an unhappy squad of players leaving for the biggest sporting event that the country had ever been involved with focused the minds of the negotiators. After an hour of negotiations in the Skylon Hotel in Drumcondra, a settlement was announced just as the team were due to leave for Italy. The players would receive bonuses retrospectively of IR£900 for each qualifying game. On top of that came the agreement that they would get a minimum of IR£400,000, or 25 per cent of the FAI's gross receipts from the World Cup itself, whichever was the larger.

The Irish team had qualified comfortably for Italia '90. In the end, their biggest scrap had been off the field with the FAI and Opel over money and contributions to the players' pool. The players used their position not just to their financial advantage, but to solidify the team spirit that Charlton had helped build within the squad.

'I've no conscience whatsoever earning money with the Irish team,' says Niall Quinn, 'because the Association earned a lot of money out of it and Opel have done great. It's not a poor Association. It's not as if there's guys in a school in the west of Ireland or somewhere who haven't got jerseys because the FAI have no money. The FAI are big business now and we feel, as Jack does, that we had some role to play in that and we should earn from it.

'Drury Communications were to ensure that we didn't overdo it, we didn't abuse the situation, we just got involved in watertight contracts usually with large companies who wanted to get involved with our name. We had foreseen this eventual possibility of success. As players we decided that if we qualified these agents would be in place, and no player would do anything, any commercial business with anybody, until after we qualified. If we got knocked out, it would look badly if we were arranging something. But if we had waited too long maybe some of the players would have gone off and agreed to do other things.

'After we qualified for Italia '90, I did one function in Dublin before the World Cup. But Kevin Moran, Frank Stapleton and Mick McCarthy were coming back every second week. They could probably have quadrupled their earnings at a very minimum at the expense of other people down the line. But they saw it as part and parcel of the team spirit and the other guys recognised that and therefore it helped create a great feeling of camaraderie.'

Chapter Ten

A Chance to be
Innocently Happy

NOBODY THOUGHT that World Cup fever would strike quite so hard, or have such violent symptoms. People were becoming delirious. Neighbours who hadn't talked for years gushingly exchanged views on Packie Bonner and penalty shoot-outs. Many were confined to pubs, where grown men could be seen weeping and wailing in front of television sets. Nobody would venture on to the streets. Mick Jagger's concert at Lansdowne Road was cancelled. So was Prince's. Dublin Bus stopped its services. An aerial view of O'Connell Street on a Monday afternoon showed it deserted. People wouldn't turn up for work and their employers stood around laughing, not seeming to care. Thousands were seen heading to the airport. There were desperate scenes there as people tried to get out. But there was no violence, just a lot of singing. Charter companies from as far away as Egypt and Jordan were flying in to help with a mass evacuation. About 30,000 had gone. The Taoiseach, Charlie Haughey, had commandeered the government jet and was leaving with senior Cabinet colleagues and members of the opposition. Movements of Irish people were spotted as far away as Australia, the States and Germany.

The diagnosis for this national illness was impossible to pinpoint. Football had grown and was no longer confined to urban areas around the country. But it certainly wasn't the national sport. Nor could people have been affected by the quality of the football they had been watching. Group F – Egypt, England, Holland and the Republic of Ireland – had been dubbed the Group of Sleep by the Italian press. Sicily and Sardinia, where the games were being played, were now The Islands of Draws. In particular, England and Ireland were the purveyors of Peasant Football. Ireland hadn't even won a game, they had all been draws.

No, it seemed to go much deeper than that.

Nell McCafferty, a feminist author and campaigner on issues particularly affecting women, was a particularly serious case. She contracted the fever in her home town, Derry, then moved down to Dublin, and brought it out with her to Italy, where she became unofficial chaplain to the thousands of fellow Irish sufferers there. She had been a keen supporter of football, but nothing like this had ever happened to her before. She was having problems coming to terms with it, and afterwards, when the fever had subsided, she tried to explain it to her friends. Her prognosis is as valid as any:

'In the early seventies, the North was fairly horrific. People were just getting killed all over the place. We were having riots everyday, you wouldn't get killed in the riots, you'd throw stones and such like. I mean, I may have enjoyed myself but it was no way to live. Alex Higgins was playing in the World Championships. We actually stopped the rioting when he was on the television and watched him playing. And you think, what a funny world, some revolutionaries we are. He was a Protestant Belfast man. I don't know whether he was nationalist or loyalist. But we enjoyed him. There was a couple of hours on the street where you knew nobody was going to get killed because Alex was playing. I was mildly interested in this aspect of what sport can do for you. Especially for boys. But the women got caught up too. I suppose because of the romance of Alex and because he was from the North and all that.

'I thought about that in the late eighties when Derry applied for the Southern League. We all need a relief from tension. Not necessarily inter-communal tension in the North but a chance to get out of ourselves. So I got caught up in getting them back into the League in a very minor way – meeting politicians and all that shite. And when Derry did get back in, we formed an Exiles club here in Dublin. And the manner in which they played when they got back in was wonderful again because they knew that everybody was terrified of us in the South; here come the Northerners, they're going to kill us if they don't win the match. And Derry played a very elaborate game. We pledged ourself to peace, before every game we'd have a band playing, we presented the opposition with gifts, showered them with crystal glass, shite like that. And we ostentatiously stood around at whatever ground we were looking peaceful. And then they were clever enough to include women. They were saying football is a family occasion, and a lot of people flocked back and women came who hadn't been involved in sport before, because some of the men made them welcome and behaved differently. And there was children there, everybody except gays. Look how nice we are.

'It was lovely for about three years and was a precursor of what the Irish fans then did for Ireland. The way the fans made a point, it became a phenomenon, that the rest of the world were hooligans but not us. Derry started that trend in the Eighties and its since been dismissed, there's no bands, no gifts, and we're bottom of the League – it fell apart. The dream ended. And that's really how I got involved in sport. I mean I went to a few matches with the Exiles club when I came to Dublin, wherever Derry was playing, we were going to all corners of Ireland. But I gave that up because you're sitting in a van with a lot of men who are farting. Who stop at every pub along the way and you don't get home till three in the morning. Let's stop at another pub. It's farting. It's peeing. It's throwing up. And they liked it. So good luck to them. It was a very small van. My life had changed. I might once have got enthusiastic about such things. They were lovely but I didn't like the smell. I didn't want to be out till three o'clock in the morning coming from Skibereen. So I fell away from the Exiles. Then I didn't get involved in sport till the World Cup last year. I didn't go over for the first games, nor had I intended to. Dunphy had made it exciting on television, the commentary was just so much better.

'The whole place was delirious. And I just flashed back to Alex Higgins and there was Ireland putting its best foot forward. After we'd been losers. I mean, look at our image abroad. I'm talking about the non-football aspect of it. Ireland is a place of killers and reactionary Catholics and all that jazz. I knew we weren't and there was another side to the story. And there we are up on the world stage – happy, charming, didn't care if we won or lost really, though it would be nice to win. Or beat them to a draw, as they say. But it was a most positive image of Ireland. We had been through the eighties in Ireland, it had been a terrible place, because we were fighting amendments on abortion, contraception and divorce. The Church had finally fought back after ten years of feminism in the seventies. The Church got up on its hind legs in the eighties and there was a civil war in this country. Politically. Families split, everybody split, it was a horrible time. We all hated each other and we kept losing. No matter which side of the referendum you were on. It was awful. Especially the abortion one. Three years of every single day front-page stories about foetuses and sperm counts. We were miserable. Absolutely miserable. And financially the country was in chaos because none of the governments had the nerve to impose what's called fiscal rectitude. Plus there was a recession. Emigration had started again, everything had started again. And there was The Troubles.

'And then suddenly the Irish team arrives. And it was a chance to be innocently happy. And that was nice for all of us who got caught up. Both to be winners, and to be charming. Winners on our terms. There was an underlying theme that these were our fellas over in England, who've suddenly then become adopted as Irish. We're sending all the young away. Brian Lenihan says the country's not big enough for them. What a horrible thing to say. We had all these Irish people abroad and we were beginning to lose touch with them. We didn't want to hear their troubles, we had so many of our own, and this was a way of linking back in with them and adopting them back again and coming to terms with the fact that to be Irish is not just to be living in Ireland, they are also abroad, a diaspora, so to speak. A diaspora that we've been losing touch with. I know from my own sister's children, she emigrated to England. We got the shock of our lives when they came home at 20; well they don't come home, they come to Ireland and told us they were English. We couldn't come to terms with that. After all the English did to us. And then one tries to be rational about it. Of course they're English, but it was still really hurtful.

'And the Irish team gave them a chance to identify with something. They're not going to get killed in England because of it, it's only football. It's nothing to do with being a Catholic, reactionary, it's nothing to do with being a Northern killer. It was just a chance to be nicely Irish, to walk the streets. And we were able to link back up with the team. And that was a huge thing in that team, the second generation. I'm sure the team didn't give a damn. They got to play international football. I suppose Billy Bingham may have been right. But as a result of playing internationally and with a team that was beginning to be adored, they may have discovered some kind of Irishness themselves, which by living in England they were forced to repress. I think no matter what their original reason, it's been a homecoming for them too, so it's just a big national warm bath of emotion, which is rationally rooted in history and in politics. It's not facile.

'And so the whole thing came together, it was lovely. It was a break. And the weather in Ireland was good too, I think that was important, it didn't even bloody rain.

'Plus we had Jack Charlton. Jack Charlton was smashing. He was truthful, honest. And that voice. I think I could listen to that man forever. We could adopt an Englishman and say, "Isn't he gorgeous?" We're not stupid, we're aware that this was a clever thing to do, but he also is in his own right. We could show the world it's not the English people we don't like, it's the British régime. I'm talking about the North now, the South would have been pretty cool about Britain too for historical reasons. Jack Charlton reminded us of all the best things that the British can do. It just makes you long for what could be, when the British are our neighbours, and we've more in common with them than we have with most people. We get along just fine with them. If the political problem was sorted out.

'The whole thing came together; the whole thing was just marvellous. I still don't know what offside means. I even took a wee bit of interest in the sport. The only thing I really understood was the goals. Or keeping them away out of our goal.

'The fans were elaborate in their courtesies, to each other and to strangers. And it allowed them to relax. Men have to learn how to relax. They're so caught up, they're worried about the dole, they're worried about hanging on to their job, they're worried about making more money in their job or promotion or whatever. If your sole identity is through your job, forget it. And this allowed them to be bigger than themselves. I like very much the men relaxing. But as one woman pointed out to me, they're relaxing at our expense. Their trips were financed at the expense of their families. We have to make economies, we have to make financial sacrifices to send them off on their holidays for six weeks every four years, so we can get a break. There was a lot of conflict. But I couldn't help it. I was so pleased. After 20 years of fighting the fuckers. To see them happy. We could even look at it in terms of every cloud has a silver lining. It gives the woman a break at home and the men are coming back happy.

'A lot of these people were in debt, behind with the mortgage, behind with the rent. Most people in Ireland don't have a disposable income. They all live in debt. Or what little disposable income they had went on their holidays, not a family holiday. But maybe Ireland's got more money than it lets on. Through the black economy. The women made sacrifices. We also enjoyed the bloody football, because you can get as much fun, or a different kind of fun, watching it on television. I was over there with the men. We were tired, dirty, sweaty, thirsty, badly sunburnt, we were worried all the time about tickets. Will we get into the matches or not? When you do see the match, you've missed half of it because people are jumping up and down, there's no such thing as an action replay. Part of me wanted to be back home saying: "I want to know what Dunphy said. I want to see the replay. I want afterwards to have a bath or a shower. I don't want to be sunburnt, I don't want to be broke." So it wasn't as if the woman at home had an awful time.

'And, you see, as usual, men are so boyish. I was amused after all the matches. Full of emotion. You know the way something wonderful happens and you want to share it with your beloved? The fuckers are all queuing up at the phones to ring back home. They didn't want to talk to each other. They wanted to talk to their wives, their mothers, their daughters, their grannies. They said things like "I love you" and I know exactly how they feel, because I was ringing home, wanting to tell somebody how much you love them.

'What surprised me also in Italy was that there was virtually no interest in sex. I thought they would all be fuckin' about. Maybe they were too shy. They didn't. They didn't go looking for it. Not that anybody wants a big red-necked Irishman. But he can get off. But he didn't. They were not interested. I find that phenomenal. The younger boys were. I met one fellow and he's married five years, he went over there. And we all arrived down in Rome. Now, there's no room in Rome. Where are you going to sleep? And this fellow ended up in the catacombs. And in the catacombs there were a few other people, one of them was a Swedish woman. And one thing led to another. And he came to me to confession the next morning and he said, "I never even thought about it. I love my wife. I was a virgin before I married my wife. What am I going to do?" He was practically in tears. And I said, "Well, did you enjoy it?" He said, "Yeah." "Consider it a bonus and go and enjoy the football." And he's the only man that I met on that whole trip who did something. I was delighted for him. You should have seen the cut of him. He was nothing, and he ends up with this big Swedish woman. He has a sexual experience in the catacombs. I said: "You know, there's people would give their right arm for what you got, including myself." He promised me he'd never do it again. On a clear day or in a discotheque you would have run by him. But in the catacombs. He was stunned that anybody could have wanted him. But he may have had a certain aura about him because we thought we were champions at that stage.

'So maybe Irish women were very wise and knew this wouldn't happen, but I'd still like an explanation. Of course, there's the classic story about Irish men that they'd crawl over 12 naked women to get their pints of stout. And we spent all our nights drinkin' and singing. We really put on the charm. It became more than football. We became conscious that we were seducing the nations of the world. And of course we got our kicks out of it. The English were getting harassed everywhere, God love them, with their Union Jacks. They were hounded, frightened and ashamed. We'd ostentatiously give them our Tricolours so that they could put them over their shoulders and get away from the hassle. Jesus, talk about goodbye Cromwell. It gave us a chance to patronise them every night. That'll change the English perception of us, so there was that undercurrent running as well. Boy, were we nice to the English.

'It was a great start to the nineties. There's not a total connection but in the nineties things have been a bit easier in Ireland, contraception was legalised, homosexuality was legalised. This has nothing to do with those men playing football, but it's all part of changing the Irish psyche. It took us out of ourselves. All these Irish people going to Italy. Another thing I loved about them was before that their idea of a holiday was a package tour. You get on a plane, you're taken to wherever you are, it could be anywhere, Ireland abroad. And then you come home again. This time a lot of them had to make their own way, by boat, train, hitchhiking. They felt like Vasco da Gama making their way around Italy. They sorted out their own hotels, train timetables, they even managed to do their own cooking. For thousands of them it was the first independent time in their lives, apart from going to England where they would have family living there or something. They felt like foreign explorers going over there, they felt like they could take on the world. One guy there had 12 different currencies on him, German marks, Dutch, dollars, he had it all sorted out and he was 21. He found his own way there from one of the roughest working-class parts of Dublin. Was he proud of himself! And in the middle of it all, when we were down in Rome, he goes off to Pompei. It had to have an element of horror. I was so proud of him, breaking out of the pack, all we wanted to do was sit around in the pub. He broke away and went away as a tourist. And a lot of boys did things like that.

'The Italians were very relaxed. I was surprised at that because I've had experiences of Carabinieri before. In Genoa we were sitting in the fountain, a three-tiered fountain, hundreds, thousands of us every night in the square, and the police just laughed. I don't know why that is. Maybe they realised that we weren't dangerous.

'If the fans saw someone who looked like he was going over the edge, they'd take him home, or sit on him or handle him. Circle him, circle the wagons. Give wee lectures about how it looks bad for the country. They minded each other a great deal, people who were broke or just too drunk. There was nothing rough or heavy about it. Say some people were drunk and looking a bit aggressive, you wouldn't fight with them, you'd joke with them. Now, I've seen other situations where Irish men would have responded differently.

'I'd never seen it before. This was what I tried to explain to the feminists when I came back home; we've got to understand this phenomenon, what makes these men behave themselves. Whatever it is, I want to tap it and give it away free on every street corner because it's done them a power of good.

'And they were nice to the women. There was no what you call sexual harassment. We had such horrific memories of travelling around in that van. It didn't happen this time.'

★

The only perceived threat to this chance to be innocently happy came from Eamon Dunphy. He had maintained that it was not simply enough to go to the World Cup. He said that Ireland could reach the semi-finals at least, and it would take a very good team to beat them. The main platform from which Dunphy expounded his views was on national television, RTE. Dunphy was a panellist along with his friend, and former team-mate and employer, John Giles, who hadn't been actively involved in the game since applying unsuccessfully for the manager's job in 1986.

For soccer coverage RTE had always had difficulty competing with the more slick presentation of BBC and ITV which were available in large parts of the country. But the presence of Giles and Dunphy on RTE – one academic and studied, the other passionate and controversial – was itself becoming a national sporting institution. When Ireland's World Cup campaign started against England, RTE had its highest ever viewing figures, about three million people, 80 per cent of the population.

A 1-1 draw against England was seen as a good start. And before the next match against Egypt, Dunphy delivered a familiar eulogy from the studios in Donnybrook, Dublin 4. 'This is for the whole nation. And the team is a catalyst. The character of our people out there, the team – they haven't had one yellow card. And the way we've celebrated. The whole thing is glorious and golden and it's for every single person, all the kids, all the players, everybody's involved and everybody's made a contribution.'

It turned out to be a terrible game, one of the worst of a bad World Cup. The Egyptians had no interest in attack and stood back while Ireland pumped a series of high balls towards Tony Cascarino. A scoreless draw meant Ireland's chance of qualifying for the next round had diminished. Back in Donnybrook, Dunphy felt that something far greater had already been lost.

'Anyone who sends a team out to play like that should be ashamed of themselves,' he said. 'We know about the upside of Jack. We know how hard these lads work. We know about their courage. But football is a two-sided game, when you haven't got the ball and when you have got the ball. When we got the ball we were cowardly, ducking out of taking responsibility.

'I feel embarrassed for soccer, embarrassed for the country, embarrassed for all the good players, for our great tradition in soccer. This is nothing to do with the players who played today. That's a good side. I feel embarrassed and ashamed of that performance, and we should be.' Dunphy finished by throwing his pen down in front of him.

It was a moment when people felt proudest to be Irish, and this was provocation of the worst kind. RTE's switchboards were jammed with complaints. Dunphy's comments were interpreted as a slur against the whole country, an impression that was compounded the next day by reports in several newspapers which quoted Dunphy as saying on television that he was ashamed to be Irish.

It then emerged that Dunphy was going out to Italy for Ireland's match against Holland. He had planned the trip months previously, but the impression given was that, having thrown down the gauntlet after Egypt, Dunphy was now travelling out to go to battle against Jack Charlton and the Irish team.

Dunphy had initially had good relations with Charlton. He stood out as the only journalist to give unequivocal support for Charlton in the manager's early period in the job, though it was expressed in typically provocative fashion. After Charlton's shaky first two months back in 1986, Dunphy had written: 'Jack Charlton's Ireland will be as stubborn as Ramsey's England and as admirably honest as he himself has been these past few weeks. Although he has upset a few people behind the scenes, posed a permanent threat to journalists who ask questions he doesn't fancy, committed an almighty blunder by picking a player he had never seen, can't remember players' names and probably wouldn't recognise the National Anthem if he heard it on the car radio, Jack Charlton has gone a long way towards proving that he is the right man for the job of managing Ireland.'

Charlton and Dunphy had dined and drank together on occasion, generally in the company of other former footballers such as Giles and Shay Brennan. But their relationship had soured after an incident at the European Championships when Charlton invited Dunphy in for dinner in the players' quarters. Dunphy told him that there were several players inside who would not be happy about sharing a table with him because of what he had written about them in the past. Among them were Stapleton, Brady and McCarthy. Charlton brushed that aside and insisted that Dunphy join him. Charlton hadn't often read Dunphy's criticisms of the players, though McCarthy had. 'I didn't read the reports,' says McCarthy, 'except that some dickhead would send them to my home half the time. In them Dunphy would say what a prat I was.' When Charlton and Dunphy walked into the players' room and sat down, Stapleton stood up and walked out. McCarthy started to follow him. 'What's the fuckin' matter with you?' Charlton asked. McCarthy said he wouldn't remain in the same room as Dunphy. Dunphy then left and the two players returned. Charlton was angry, but the players explained to him why they had embarrassed him in front of his guest.

As the players were returning from Germany, Dunphy launched his fiercest attack yet on McCarthy in the *Sunday Independent*. The paper was handed out to the players on the plane. Charlton was reading the article when McCarthy leaned over his shoulder. 'I don't think you should see this,' Charlton said to him, 'it'll ruin your day.' McCarthy insisted and Charlton then apologised to him for having inflicted Dunphy on him back in the hotel in Hanover.

At the airport hotel, Charlton spotted Dunphy. 'I got hold of him, and I said: "You, you little cunt. I tell you something. I've gone along with you and I've tried to help you. But now you can fuck off. 'Cos I'm joining their fucking ranks. I want fuck all to do with you."'

And that was where they left it, until Dunphy came over to Italy before the game against Holland. Charlton had heard about all the fuss at home about Dunphy's remarks after the Egypt game, but had dismissed it as a minor irritant. Dunphy turned up at a press conference that Charlton was giving. He wanted to ask Charlton a question: if the way of playing in the qualifying matches for the World Cup and in the actual event should be different . . . Charlton interrupted. 'You're not allowed to ask a question,' he said. Dunphy wanted to know why and Charlton responded, 'Because you're not a proper journalist.' Dunphy pointed out that he was there representing the *Sunday Independent*. Charlton said that everyone else present was interested in football, 'so you're not a proper journalist. We're not answering questions from you.' With that Charlton walked off, saying he would talk to five senior journalists back at the team hotel.

There were immediate recriminations once Charlton had left the room, with lines drawn roughly between the English journalists, who defended Dunphy's right to ask questions, and their Irish counterparts, most of whom had long tired of Dunphy's abrasive style and were annoyed at missing their chance to get some information out of the manager. Peter Byrne of the *Irish Times*, who had been commissioned to write a Jack Charlton diary of the World Cup, said that the manager was doing the journalists a favour by holding a press conference in the first place. The argument grew quite heated; at one stage, Cathal Dervan of the Irish edition of the *Star*, told Ian Ridley of the *Guardian* to 'fuck off back to England'.

Incredibly, with about 15,000 Irish supporters in Italy, this was one of the most acrimonious incidents. Otherwise it was one long celebration. Bonner's save in the penalty shootout against Romania and O'Leary's winning strike marked its emotional climax. After losing 1-0 to the hosts Italy in the quarter-finals, both players and fans faced the journey home in a state of exhaustion. As the Aer Lingus 737, renamed Saint Jack for the occasion, approached Dublin, the captain made an announcement. 'I am changing the route slightly,' he said. 'We are going to fly in over O'Connell Street and I want everybody to look out.' The passengers fell silent, as below they could see tens of thousands of people on the street bedecked in green. Fifty thousand Germans gathered to welcome home their victorious World Cup side. In Dublin that Sunday afternoon, about 300,000 people were on the streets waiting for one of the teams that had been knocked out in the quarter-finals.

On the ground in Dublin, Charlton watched in terror as children ran beside the wheels of the open-topped bus that carried the players to the centre of the town. He shouted and screamed at them to move out of the way. At a public reception in the centre of town, he gestured to the crowd to quieten down as they jeered a couple of politicians who were making speeches from the podium. And at the end of the evening he told the crowd to disperse slowly and calmly. He was the master of ceremonies. He was completely in control.

★

Charlton might also have fixed a disapproving glare on the politicians from all parties engaged in an undignified struggle with each other to get one of the seats on the platform with the football heroes. Successive governments had shunned the game of soccer in Ireland, starving it of any grants or official recognition and had allowed the GAA to bully soccer, which helped keep it in the doldrums for so long.

The Taoiseach, Charles Haughey, who had done his own lap of honour of the Olympic Stadium after the defeat against Italy in the quarter-finals, had also been at Dublin airport to deliver a welcoming speech. It was political opportunism of the purest form. In the past, Haughey had consistently turned down invitations from the FAI to attend matches at Lansdowne Road, afraid to upset the powerful GAA lobby.

The GAA had been founded in 1884 to help forge the cultural and sporting side of the nationalist movement that was gaining strength in Ireland at the time. Its basic aim, as it stated, was the strengthening of national identity in a 32-county Ireland through the presentation and promotion of Gaelic games. As part of its brief, it invoked a rule banning GAA players and officials from playing or attending any 'foreign' games – principally rugby and soccer. The rule was strictly enforced in schools run by the Christian Brothers who took on the weight of responsibility of primary and secondary education throughout the country.

Some of Ireland's most prominent older soccer players had to run the gauntlet of angry Christian Brothers to play their favoured sport at the weekend. Ray Treacy was expelled from Westland Row school at the age of 14 for fighting with a teacher who had beaten him for playing soccer with a club side at the weekend instead of playing for the school Gaelic football team. His team-mate Eoin Hand took the beatings and played both Gaelic football and soccer, but his form of punishment was to be denied a Dublin Minor Championship medal when he was a member of the winning team.

A GAA activist, Tom Woulfe, took exception to the rule in the sixties when he found that he couldn't watch his son play rugby for Terenure College for fear of being informed on by the spies who had taken it upon themselves to enforce the ban.

After a long campaign led by Woulfe, the ban was repealed in 1971. Players such as Packie Bonner, Kevin Moran and Niall Quinn would in future play both codes, and excel at both, without fear of official retribution.

While the ban was removed, the hostile attitude towards soccer by the GAA authorities remained as strong as ever. It was forbidden for soccer to be played on GAA pitches or any other part of GAA property – this particular ban was subjected to close scrutiny in 1994 when an Under-11 side was prevented from playing indoor soccer on GAA premises in Co Wicklow.

The virulent campaign against soccer had its effect. Even in urban areas, where soccer had a hold, it often lost out to the GAA. On top of that, the GAA was a superbly run organisation at local level, providing free equipment for its players, transport to games, hot showers and a social scene that became a focal point for many towns and villages. International soccer has always been able to draw big crowds in Dublin, but soccer remained a pursuit for the minority. Generations never discovered the simple pleasures of a Sunday afternoon kickaround. 'It was a fourth, fifth, or tenth rated sport,' Mick McCarthy discovered when he came to Ireland. 'There was hurling, Gaelic football, the horses, probably the dogs, and I should imagine darts and dominoes.'

But the GAA's hold over the country's sporting pursuits had long become a fragile one, dating from the 1970 World Cup, when television beamed in fantastic colour pictures of eleven yellow-clad Brazilians engaged in a sublime display of sporting artistry against Italy. It was somewhat deceiving – many in Ireland thought that game was a standard international football match and have been waiting decades to see its like again. Ireland sat, watched and admired while every four years other countries took part in the biggest and most glamorous sporting show on earth. Gaelic games had a missing dimension – in forging its own national game, the GAA had by extension cut itself off from the rest of the world. That was a minor consideration in 1884, but by the latter part of this century the thirst for international competition was one that the GAA couldn't satisfy. The only outlets were games against Australian Rules Football sides, where the two Associations would first have to decide whether to play with the round or the oval ball.

The success of the international football side has ruptured the GAA heartland. After Italia '90 figures released by the FAI showed that the number of registered soccer players had nearly doubled – from 80,000 to 140,000 – in the four years since Charlton had become manager. As well as increases in the established soccer centres such as Cork City, Limerick, Waterford, Sligo and Galway, there had also been spectacular increases in areas such as Mayo, Clare, Kerry and Tipperary.

The League of Ireland, or National League as it is now called, has struggled to exploit the international team's success and the huge increase in soccer participation. For any teenager with serious ambitions to be a professional footballer, the route still leads to apprenticeship schemes in England. The most promising development for domestic soccer in Ireland has been switching from Sunday afternoon to Friday evening. This has been made possible by the provision of floodlights at many grounds, funded by a deal the FAI made with Sky Television, in which it received IR£1,500,000 to allow the satellite channel to beam English Premier League Football live into the country. Attendances at some grounds have trebled because of the Friday evening fixtures.

However, at club level, most supporters have clung to their loyalty to Gaelic football. Shamrock Rovers paid a terrible price for the antipathy of their fans and the rest of the community towards domestic soccer. After Giles resigned as manager of Rovers in 1983, Jim McLaughlin, the most successful manager in the League of Ireland, took over. With the Kilcoynes continuing to inject money into the club, McLaughlin enjoyed spectacular success, winning the League for three years running and the FAI Cup twice in those same years. Attendances at Milltown had increased at the beginning of McLaughlin's period as manager, but dwindled amidst widespread apathy at Rovers' success. For the Kilcoyne brothers, this was the last straw. They decided to recoup the money they had invested in Rovers in the best way they could. They announced that Rovers were moving out of Milltown, their home since 1926. Attempts by a group of supporters to buy the ground from the Kilcoynes failed. Their offer didn't come close to the IR£900,000 which the Kilcoynes eventually received from property developers for the sale of the ground. After lengthy planning objections, Milltown, widely regarded as the best ground in the League of Ireland, was razed to make way for a housing estate. Louis Kilcoyne defended the decision to sell the ground as the only way his family could recover the million pounds it had pumped into the club in the previous 15 years. Rovers eventually found a new home at the RDS horse showjumping grounds in Ballsbridge. Players must be inoculated against Equine TB before joining the club.

The bitter wrangling over the sale of Milltown would re-emerge when Kilcoyne was elected President of the FAI. 'We think it's a kick in the teeth for Rovers from the other clubs,' says Rovers' new owner John McNamara. 'It's like as if Martin Edwards sold Old Trafford and houses were put on it, Manchester United were moved to Maine Road, and Martin Edwards was appointed Secretary or Chief Executive of the English Premier League.'

It was the sight of those politicians scrambling to get on the Italia '90 bandwagon, as Milltown was being sacrificed to the property developers, that sickened many Rovers fans. But Italia '90, for some, was as much a chance to get snouts in the trough as it was for celebrations. In the feel-good atmosphere that followed, there was the extraordinary spectacle of a testimonial being pushed through for the outgoing FAI President, Fran Fields, whose pig business in Donegal had run into difficulties. Twenty thousand people turned up at Dalymount Park to see Ireland beat Morocco 1-0, many of them unwitting benefactors to the IR£55,000 that went to Fields from the game. There was a precedent here, in the testimonial awarded to the outgoing general secretary, P.J O'Driscoll, in 1988, immediately after the European Championships.

The granting of testimonials, not just for officials but for players, has now got out of hand. Ireland is one of the few countries to latch on to the idea of the international testimonial, and the queue of potential recipients gets longer by the day. The wily old triumvirate – Stapleton, O'Leary and Brady have squeezed through theirs. The former Irish midfielder, Gerry Daly, who was supposed to have a testimonial more than ten years ago, was amazed to get a telephone call from David O'Leary saying he had his testimonial organised and could he go ahead in front of him. Kevin Moran is the latest player to avail himself of a testimonial, earning an estimated £200,000 from a game against a Kenny Dalglish Eleven. Moran is one of the most popular players ever to pull on a green shirt but, unlike players from other eras, has been well rewarded financially for his years with Ireland. Moran it was who was one of the players who put the matter of playing for Ireland on a sound business footing, with high financial rewards to accompany the honour of playing for one's country. Payments to players – of one million pounds – took up three-quarters of the money the FAI received from FIFA for USA '94.

Friendly games, a vital source of income for the FAI in its efforts to promote the game in Ireland, are difficult to slot in amidst the competitive fixtures and the players' club commitments. That they be taken up on a regular basis with testimonials for players or officials is, at this stage, an abuse of the goodwill of the Irish supporter and a shameless exploitation of power and influence.

The players argue that theirs is a short career full of financial uncertainties, as though the rest of us were all safely ensconced in guaranteed jobs-for-life. They seem to have forgotten that they themselves were nurtured in schoolboy leagues and amateur clubs still in need of constant financial up-keep and still run by the same men who never expected any financial return for the investment they were making.

The subject of money is one which the players are deeply sensitive about. Sports journalists working with the Irish team who have written about payments to players have been taken aside and warned about their access to the team being put in jeopardy. As a result, the journalists often write the stories without a byline or the information is buried down at the end of the piece. Ironically, the biggest earner of them all in the Irish set-up, Charlton, is the one least hung-up about it. Money was the last thing on Charlton's mind when he took the job. For the first year, his salary and that of his assistant, Maurice Setters (though he only worked half the year), plus their expenses, came to only IR£45,000. But as the team's stock increased – and Charlton became the most charismatic figure in the land – he was quick to seize the opportunity to make some big money. There were weeks when Charlton would have no commitments with the Irish team, and he would tour the country, making after-dinner speeches, opening supermarkets, endorsing products. Charlton was able to charge around IR£3,000 for an afternoon's work. Between that and his television advertising campaigns for big companies such as Bank of Ireland and Avonmore Dairies, Charlton's annual income has gained an extra couple of noughts, to about half a million pounds.

In his local pub in Dublin, Hill 16, Charlton was being ribbed by the regulars about an article in that night's *Evening Herald* setting out his huge earnings. Charlton's initial response put the little episode on a comic footing: 'I haven't got me glasses with me, lend me yours,' he said to an old man at the bar drinking a pint of Guinness. Charlton was able to focus with the borrowed spectacles and spent a silent minute reading the article, watched by the pub. Then he looked up, handed the glasses back and proclaimed indignantly, 'Don't they realise that I pay 40 per cent tax on all that?' The drinks were on the house.

Chapter Eleven

BYDGOSCSH BANISHED

SPAIN. IRELAND REP. DENMARK. N IRELAND. ALBANIA. LITHUANIA. LATVIA. The Group 3 draw for the qualifying round of the 1994 World Cup would provide the FAI with the opportunity to show that it had followed the lead of its team in changing itself into a tightly knit, highly professional outfit. It was not the quality of the opposition that caused the greatest worries, rather the logistics of competing in a seven-nation group that would take the team from Madrid to Tirana and then over to the new European frontier countries, Latvia and Lithuania. And in the end, the greatest test of the team's mettle was to come from a trip within the island of Ireland itself, one hundred miles up the road from Dublin to Windsor Park, in circumstances that neither the FAI nor anybody else has been able to come to terms with.

The first victory of the campaign was achieved in Copenhagen in January 1992 when the FAI negotiators met their group counterparts to thrash out the schedule for the groups. Charlton and the FAI President, Michael Hyland, got what they were looking for – away games against the two toughest teams in the group, Denmark and Spain, in the early part of the domestic league season in Britain, when their players were still fresh and eager. In the event Ireland were unlucky to only draw both matches. Their midfield dominated, with Roy Keane showing that he was emerging as a player of genuine international stature.

Ireland's first match of the group had been played a few months previously at home to Albania, a country which had just rejoined the international community after 40 years of isolation under the old Communist government. The arrival of the Albanian team in Dublin was a portent of what the Irish team could expect when they travelled to Tirana for the return fixture. The Albanian party arrived at Dublin airport with no money, no strip, no music sheet for their new National Anthem and only half their senior squad. The Albanians received a loan from the FAI, underwritten by FIFA, and the donation of a strip by Adidas. Faced with the prospect of having to play half their Under-21 side which was also on the trip, an Albanian official waited at Dublin airport for the remaining members of the squad, who were stranded at Athens airport because nobody had paid for their tickets. They eventually arrived the day before the match, and Albania was able to field a reasonably strong side, but Ireland dominated the match and won 2-0.

The return match in Tirana had the makings of another Bydgoscsh. Northern Ireland had had a torrid experience there. They were delayed for hours at the airport because of red tape and, in the middle of winter, there had been no hot water and frequent power cuts.

Charlton had travelled with the Northern Ireland team to spy on the opposition and to assess the problems which his team might experience off the field. He had learned from Revie the importance of proper preparation. 'You've got to look after the players,' he says, 'pay attention to detail, inform the players about everything that is necessary, make sure their is no stone unturned for the players and travel in the best possible way. You look after the players because they are the important people.' Charlton had a room on the tenth floor of the Hotel Tirana. Outside, the Northern Ireland captain, Alan McDonald, was stuck in the lift. Charlton had walked up to his room in darkness, and was there with his own supply of salmon and chicken and game pie. 'It's the sort of place you get into as late as possible,' he said. 'You bring your own grub, get up, go for a walk, play the game and get out. I'll find the worst pitch in Ireland to prepare for this match.'

When the Republic made the trip there months after Charlton had hitched a ride with the northern team, they were well prepared. Each member of the travelling party was given a kit containing a roll of toilet paper, a candle, a towel, a bar of soap and a bottle of mineral water. Two chefs travelled with the party bringing their own ingredients, pots, pans, cooking oil and washing-up liquid. An Irish officer with the United Nations in Tirana, Lieutenant Colonel Wally Hayes, chipped in, organising a translator, helping to block book the hotel and arranging for the swift passage of the team through Customs. Ireland came from a goal behind to win 2-1.

It had been a clinical performance both on and off the field. The only blemish was that another of Charlton's centre halves had decided to go on holiday rather than turn up for the match. Paul McGrath, the rock of nearly every Irish team performance, was showing himself to have the constitution of a Humpty Dumpty out in the real world.

The team had gathered in Dublin on Sunday afternoon, three days before flying out to Albania. On Monday morning Charlton received a message from an employee at the team hotel that someone had telephoned to say that McGrath would not be travelling to Tirana because of an injury to his knee. McGrath's knees were bothering him alright, as they had been for years, but the immediate cause of his absence was his other career-threatening affliction, the vodka bottle. McGrath had been drinking heavily for years. His behaviour was a disturbing reminder of the decline of that other great black Dubliner, Phil Lynott.

In Manchester, the pub crawls of McGrath and his teammate, Norman Whiteside, were celebrated. He had lived up to the stereotype of the flawed footballing genius by crashing his car through three front gardens after one such binge. Both Whiteside and McGrath were struggling with serious injuries, though in McGrath's case his problems were compounded by a turbulent personal life. Raised in orphanages in Dublin for much of his early life, McGrath hadn't adapted well to family life when it finally arrived. Marriage and three sons hadn't stopped McGrath living the life of a bachelor and his relationship with his wife had deteriorated to the point where she had been admitted to hospital suffering from depression.

A week before the Albania game McGrath had travelled with his new girlfriend to Cork where he was doing a coaching session for local children and a question and answer session in a pub in the town of Crosshaven. Instead of returning to Dublin as scheduled on Saturday night, McGrath, cranking up on one of his binges, had booked into the Crosshaven Hotel and had then gone to the dog races in Cork. On Tuesday, as the Irish team were flying out to Albania, McGrath was at Cork airport catching a flight himself, to Birmingham. Harried by a group of reporters, he boarded an aircraft bound for London before being directed on to the right flight. 'My dodgy knees are keeping me out of this particular match,' he told the media. 'I just hope people believe me when I say that.' From Birmingham, McGrath flew to Israel where he and his girlfriend had booked into a holiday resort near Tel Aviv by the time his team-mates were taking the field in Tirana.

It was the second important game that McGrath had missed for Ireland in such a fashion. Three years previously, after being fêted over his performances in Italia '90, McGrath had gone on a week-long binge in Dublin before a European Championship qualifying game against Turkey. McGrath had arrived back in the team hotel the night before the match after being tracked down by the physiotherapist, Mick Byrne, but he developed the shakes on the coach on the way to the match and had to be sent back to the hotel. The press – Dunphy included! – had regurgitated Charlton's explanation that McGrath had initially missed training because he had been given permission to see his mother who was ill, and had then missed the match itself because of the old knee injury.

With the co-operation of the press, Charlton had been able to cover up that incident, but he hadn't made any excuses for McGrath's profligate behaviour for the game against Albania. He had simply commented publicly that he didn't know where Paul McGrath was, though his guess, made in private, was spot on. 'He's probably off in a hotel room somewhere with some bird and a bottle of vodka,' Charlton said. 'It makes me so fucking angry. There are people in this country who are supposed to look after Paul, his so-called friends. Instead, they seem happier leading him astray.'

From Tel Aviv, McGrath had finally contacted Charlton and was told to come to Dublin, where the team was now preparing for David O'Leary's testimonial game against Hungary.

McGrath's absence from the Albania game, and his general mental condition, was the most sensitive problem that Charlton had to face in his seven years as manager of the Irish team. He was aware of the public perception that O'Leary had been exiled from the Irish team for more than two years for missing an inconsequential tournament in Iceland so that he could go on a pre-booked holiday with his family. But, as Charlton had tired of explaining, O'Leary was surplus to his requirements. McGrath was central to them. 'I hope to meet Paul as soon as possible to talk things over,' he said. 'After all, we're speaking here of the best player in Britain and a valuable member of our World Cup squad.'

Charlton again showed a deftness of touch that belied his forthright and tough image. After speaking to a number of senior players, he berated McGrath and then left it at that. 'Paul only started to let us down in the last couple of years,'

Charlton said. 'Before that he was as good as gold. Granted, over the past 18 months his position has got worse and worse and worse, and I don't know if it's his injuries or what it is. He's a special case and we need to look after him. The lads knew how important he was to the team, he's such a good player. And if they help to keep him right, they were prepared to go along with that. And to be fair, not one person spoke out of line about Paul, and we knew his problems for 18 months, two years. But we kept it in-house. It helped build team spirit because the lads got together and they said, "We need Paul, so we've got to look after him." My decision to keep him on was simply that if Paul McGrath turns up and is fit and is great, he's your best player.'

After Albania, Ireland's next games in the qualifying round began two weeks later in the Baltic states. McGrath was picked and scored in a 2-0 victory over Latvia, and Ireland then beat Lithuania 1-0 in Vilnius.

Unlike Ireland, Spain and Denmark had faltered in their visits to the Baltics. As a result Ireland were in the comfortable position of being able to qualify for the World Cup if they beat Spain in their second-last game of the group. Lansdowne Road was packed with supporters who had come for a party as much as a football match, such was the confidence that the Irish side would beat even such talented opposition as Spain. The crowd was stunned after five minutes when Spain scored, and there was an eerie, uneasy silence for the rest of the game as the classy Spanish side scored two more goals and eventually won the game by 3-1. It was a big wobble by the Irish side. Billy Bingham, the Northern Irish manager, was desperate to supply the knock-out punch.

★

The Irish Football Association in Belfast. The Football Association of Ireland in Dublin. To an outsider, there's obviously something funny going on here. Many Irish people can't understand it either. Of the 48 sports regulated in Ireland, only three others are divided along the same lines as the football associations.

The split is a sporting manifestation of the religious and political divides in the country. Its origins go back to the latter part of the previous century when football became an organised sport in Ireland as well as elsewhere. Southern and northern teams played in the same league then, the Irish League, and the international side played under the one organisation, the Irish Football Association. But matches between clubs were often interrupted by fighting between rival supporters whose club allegiancies were forged along religious lines.

The flashpoint for the divide came in 1921, the year after the Irish Free State, as the Republic of Ireland was then known, gained limited independence from Britain. The Dublin club, Shelbourne, had reached the semi-final of the Irish FA Cup against a northern side, Glenavon. The IFA insisted that the match and a subsequent replay both be played in Belfast, despite the objections of Shelbourne. It was interpreted as a snub to the southern clubs and other clubs in Dublin were also incensed at the IFA's ruling that football couldn't be played on a Sunday. That year a group of eight clubs in the South met and agreed to form the Football Association of Ireland. Several clubs from Catholic areas of Belfast and Derry also joined the new Association. The FAI was admitted to FIFA in 1923, which meant it could now stage internationals. The IFA had attempted to block recognition, but now the Associations came to an arrangement. At a meeting in Liverpool, it was established that the FAI should confine itself to the 26 counties of the Irish Free State and that the two bodies should recognise each other's suspensions of players.

Since then Northern Ireland, as the IFA was eventually forced to call its national side, has enjoyed more success historically than the Republic. The team had qualified for three World Cups – 1958, 1982 and 1986 – before the Republic had reached a single one. Billy Bingham had played as a winger for

Northern Ireland in 1958, and he became manager in 1980. Apart from staunch nationalist circles, both communities in the North celebrated the success of Bingham's team in reaching the quarter finals in Spain in 1982. This was helped by the fact that half the team, including Northern Ireland's most capped player, Pat Jennings, team captain Martin O'Neill, and the top scorer, Gerry Armstrong, were Catholics. Support from the nationalist community in the North was also forthcoming as the Republic's international side found it impossible to break on to the world stage. In Dublin there was also general support for the North as it enjoyed its spell of success, coupled with consistent calls that the sport be united under an all-Ireland international team.

The pendulum swung south of the border after 1986 when Bingham's ageing side broke up, to be replaced by young players mostly from the lower divisions of the English Leagues, and Charlton took over the manager's job in the Republic. Drawn in the same group in the qualifying round for Italia '90, the Republic qualified comfortably ahead of the North.

That same scenario was unfolding in the qualifying round for USA '94. The Republic were already in a strong position coming into their home game in March 1993 against Northern Ireland while their opponents were struggling. Charlton didn't bother to disguise his lack of anxiety about the fixture. 'Let me put it this way,' Charlton said, 'I won't be losing any sleep about the match against them in Dublin. I'm not exactly in a flap about Northern Ireland.'

Bingham took exception to Charlton's remarks: 'Jack is being presumptuous and premature and you can't do that in football. You can never predict how a match between the Irish will turn out.' Later, Bingham, as much a populist as Charlton, put his side's chances in more ringing terms. He talked of striking 'the fear of God into the Republic'. 'My paupers,' he said, 'can trip up Big Jack's princes at Lansdowne.'

By half time, however, Northern Ireland looked truly impoverished. They were 3-0 down to a steamrolling Republic side and the second half passed without any further goals being scored. It was a crushing defeat for Bingham's team which virtually ended their chances of qualifying for USA '94. To rub salt into the wounds, a large section of the Lansdowne Road crowd took up a chant of 'One team in Ireland' to the tune of *Guantanamera*. Normally a fairly benign refrain, it took on a triumphalist edge in the context of relations between the North and South. It was also cutting to Bingham and the players because it was a crude way of expressing the truth – that the Republic were now in a different class to the North.

By the time the Republic came to Windsor Park for their last match of the qualifying group, they needed at least a point to go through, while Northern Ireland were already out of it. The team were, however, in the true sense of the words, playing for their pride. It was Bingham's last match after 14 years as manager. The notion that, after all that time, there was only one team in Ireland, and it wasn't his, rankled. Two days before the game Bingham gave notice that his team had serious reason to put one over on the Republic. 'It hurts badly when I think back to what happened to us in Dublin last season. A reporter asked me what I thought about the crowd chanting about there being only one team in Ireland. I told him there was just a chance that, come the return match, our supporters would be taunting their visitors in similar fashion with the tune of "You were never born in Ireland." At least our team is of Irish extraction and our players are not mercenaries.'

Of the squad of 21 selected by Charlton for the game, only six were born in Ireland. The presence in the Republic's side of the Manchester City centre half, Alan Kernaghan, particularly upset the IFA. Kernaghan's grandparents on his father's side had been born in Belfast and his parents now lived in Bangor. Kernaghan himself, having lived in Bangor for much of his youth, had been capped six times as a schoolboy international for Northern Ireland. Since then, however, he had been ignored by Northern Ireland and while playing for Middlesbrough had been drafted into the Republic's side by Charlton.

The mercenary remarks were greeted with fury south of the border and became the focal point for the animosity which surrounded the game. Bingham appeared to be appealing to the worst, and most vocal, constituency within the group of Northern Ireland supporters who were now in the ascendancy. They called themselves Billy's Boys. With the break up of the Catholic "old guard" within the team in 1986, a group of loyalist supporters began to direct sectarian abuse at players brought in from the nationalist community, who were made scapegoats for the team's failure. The defender, Anton Rogan, was picked out because he was a west Belfast Catholic and played for Glasgow Celtic. Sports researchers, John Sugden and Alan Bairner, at the University of Ulster, have noticed that the renewed association of loyalist extremism with the Northern Ireland team has alienated many Catholics, who found it psychologically and physically threatening to visit Windsor Park. They say that this Catholic exodus has been accompanied by a gradual drift away by more liberal-minded Protestants who have been turned off both by their team's performance and the sectarianism of sections of the crowd there.

Furthermore, the bad feeling engendered between the two camps had come at a particularly bad time as there was already a mood of deep apprehension surrounding the fixture at Windsor Park created by far more serious problems than those surrounding a game of football. In the weeks before the fixture there had again been a sharp escalation in violence. The IRA had blown up a butcher's shop in the Protestant heartland of the Shankill Road in Belfast, killing ten people. In the week that followed, Loyalist gunmen had shot dead 13 people around the North, including seven in a pub in the village of Greysteel. FIFA, the FAI and the IFA had met in Zurich, amid reports that the venue for the game was going to be switched to England to avoid the possibility that the match in Belfast might lead to further violence. After further meetings between FIFA and the IFA it was confirmed that the match would go ahead in Belfast.

In a similar arrangement to the fixture at Lansdowne Road, only 400 tickets had been issued by the FAI to the Republic's fans travelling to Belfast. Nonetheless, it was reported that several thousand were planning to travel. Newspapers in the Republic ran stories advising fans about the best route to take, and background information for those still intending to go to the game.

The Republic's squad had been based in their regular retreat in the Nuremore Hotel in Monaghan close to the border with Northern Ireland. Rather than take the short journey by coach to the ground, they returned to Dublin and flew up to Belfast. The game kicked off at eight p.m. the same time as the other deciding fixture between Spain and Denmark. At stake were the two qualifying places for the World Cup, and to be sure of qualification, the Republic had to win. A defeat would mean that they would go out. The Northern crowd did its best to intimidate the opposition by fair means or foul. It roared out *God Save the Queen* before the match; as at Lansdowne only one anthem was played. A section of the crowd then targeted certain Irish players as the game got under way. Terry Phelan and Paul McGrath were subjected to racist abuse, Kernaghan was 'a Fenian traitor'. As widely expected, the first half was tense, scoreless and scrappy. At half-time it was 0-0, the same scoreline as in Seville. If the scores stayed that way, the Republic would go out.

The Republic started off the second half in better style; Cascarino them came to the touchline, shouting a message that Spain had scored; at this rate the Republic and Spain would go through. Then disaster in the shape of Jimmy Quinn struck. With his two legs in the air, he hit a sweet volley from the edge of the area that flew into the net to the left of Packie Bonner. Billy Bingham did a dance of delight on the touchline and then turned to Charlton and yelled, 'Does it feel a bit like déjà vu, Jack?' He then looked up at the stand and began conducting the crowd. 'One team in Ireland,' they roared. 'There's only one team in Ireland.'

'Jack was twelve minutes from going fishing,' a wistful Bingham said afterwards.

That was until the Republic's substitute Alan McLoughlin took a clearance on his chest on the edge of the area and volleyed low into the right-hand corner of the net in the 78th minute. The game finished in a 1-1 draw and the attention now switched to Seville, where there were four minutes of play left. Spain were playing with ten men as their goalkeeper, Zubizarreta, had been sent off in the first half. But they held out for a 1-0 victory, and Spain and the Republic went through.

Chapter Twelve

THE HUNT FOR JASON MCATEER

AT A PRESS CONFERENCE after the game, Bingham was asked by journalists from Dublin whether he would now withdraw his remarks about mercenaries. He refused and instead asked the reporters, 'Don't you know who they are?'

Later Bingham admitted that he had made the comments as 'part of the psychological warfare that goes on between managers'. But he said that his accusation nonetheless had a good foundation. 'There was no anti-Republican feeling from me, because I'm not that way. But there was an anti-Jack feeling, I'll be honest with you. I felt, if he had licence to rubbish us, I had licence to say things about his team.

'He put out the bait first of all and I accepted it. He didn't like what he got back because there's a big grain of truth in what I say. A lot of people in the Republic don't like it. But if they examine it thoroughly, they'll see the truth.

'There are fellas playing for the Republic with very tenuous strands of qualification. Some of them hadn't even been to Ireland before they played for you. What do they feel for Ireland? I went down that road once with Lawrie Sanchez of Wimbledon, but I soon found that he had no real feeling for the North, and I took him out of it very quickly. It wasn't his fault, bless him. He wanted to play. But he hadn't got that nationalist feeling that you need. When you feel that you're playing for the flag, you're playing for the shirt, you're playing for these people, you want to lay your life down for them. I did that as a player. I felt that. And I just didn't see how he could feel that.

'I think this could apply to some of the players with the Republic. Not all, of course. There will be a big percentage for whom the feeling is very strong. But I think "mercenaries" is a good description of the others.'

The Republic's team members found it particularly ironic that Bingham should be bandying about the term 'mercenary'. Some, like Niall Quinn, dismissed his comments as a bit of gamesmanship. Others, like McGrath, were less forgiving. 'If he wants to make that allegation to my face, I know exactly what I'll do.'

Regardless of motivation, Charlton's criteria for picking players is very simple. 'If a player is quality, I'll use him,' he says. 'When I took over the job and there were all these mutterings about an Englishman getting the job and I would bring all the, you know, and then when I got John Aldridge and a couple of others, a lot of the press lads wrote nasty little things, and I remember saying to them, "Now, wait a minute, you want me to compete with the best in the world, I've got to have the fuckin' best in the world. And it's not here in Ireland that I can find it, I've got to go to England to find it, or to Scotland to find the quality that will make you a team that can compete with the best in the world. Now, if you don't want to do that, tell me, and I'll fuckin' concentrate on the League of Ireland and we'll win nothing. But give me the freedom to produce results and I will produce results." The general consensus was, "Yeah, we want to get results, all the Irish people want to get results." They were sick of the Irish team not getting results.

'Billy Bingham says we've got all fuckin' – what was the terminology he used? – mercenaries. We've got three or four, but we haven't got that many. Most of our lads are Irish-born and bred. We haven't got a team of eleven fucking great-grandmothers. We've used the law that says we can do something, that is the same law in England, Scotland and Northern Ireland. And England have, Scotland have, so why does Billy suddenly make us fuckin' mercenaries? Billy had the same opportunity and he decided not to, that's his choice.'

Undeterred by Bingham's comments Charlton announced bluntly after Windsor Park that the recruitment drive would not only continue, but would be stepped up. 'We've got one or two players who are getting past their sell-by dates,' Charlton said. 'Although they all want to play, I know we have got to get a few younger lads in the side and give them an opportunity to prove what they can do.'

Charlton was helped by a ruling by FIFA introduced in June 1993 which significantly liberalised the rules on eligibility. Previously FIFA prohibited a player from representing one country if he had already played an international of any description for another. The new ruling states that, 'Any player who is qualified to play for more than one national association will be deemed to have committed himself to one association only when he plays his first international match in an official competition [at any level] for that association.' This means that international friendlies and B internationals are no longer being taken into consideration by FIFA.

Ray Houghton, Kevin Moran, John Aldridge and Packie Bonner were seen as the players most threatened by Charlton's observations about sell-by dates, and there followed a bout of speculation about their possible replacements. The Nottingham Forest striker, Stan Collymore, was one of the first names mentioned. The story ran in the Irish newspapers before being killed off crudely by the Forest manager, Frank Clark: 'Stan Collymore assures me that the nearest he ever came to being Irish was drinking a half pint of Guinness.'

The Leeds goalkeeper, Mark Beeney, conducted a thorough investigation of his lineage but could only establish that his great-grandmother, an O'Connor, was born in Ireland. The Arsenal centre half, Andy Linighan, who had rejected an approach by Jack Charlton in the past and played for England in a B international against Ireland, was happy to see his name put forward again. 'Jack knows that I'm still available and I would be very interested to hear from him. It's every player's dream to play in the World Cup.'

The sudden spate of claims from Linighan and others provoked a reaction from his one time team-mate and fellow central defender, David O'Leary, who was still hoping himself for a place in Charlton's World Cup squad. 'I wonder about this development,' he said. 'I think we lose face by paying attention to these claims of Irishness. You have people like the Linighans suddenly interested in playing for the Republic. They weren't before when they had the chance to play for England. Suddenly we have people with virtually no feeling for Ireland wanting to muscle in. I find that in the last few months the whole idea of declaring for Ireland has become a big joke.'

Charlton, however, had no such qualms. When it emerged from Joe Kinnear at Wimbledon that his striker Dean Holdsworth had some Irish ancestry, Charlton was quick to act. Charlton was on other business at the time when he read about the Holdsworth story in the newspapers. He was on his way to Sligo, as part of his contract with the Bank of Ireland, to do a lunchtime talk for businessmen and sign autographs at a local tennis club. Initially, Charlton was somewhat puzzled by the emergence of Holdsworth. 'I've seen him play,' he said, 'but I never watched him in the context of playing for the Irish, so I'm not sure what he's like.' At the hotel just outside Sligo town, as Charlton relaxed before his luncheon appointment, he discussed the Holdsworth story with a group of sports journalists with whom he had accidentally crossed paths. Their enthusiasm for Holdsworth concentrated Charlton's mind. While being driven around the town and the nearby Lough Gill by a bank official, Charlton asked could he use the mobile telephone in the car. He rang the FAI in Dublin. 'Hello,' he said, 'it's Jack here. I want you to tell Sean [*Connolly, the General Secretary*] to get on to Maurice Setters and tell Maurice to contact Joe Kinnear to say we're interested in the lad . . . what's his name? Holdsworth. Dean Holdsworth. Have you got that? . . . Good. Thanks, luv. Bye.'

Holdsworth was due to play in a B international for England, but this didn't seem to bother Charlton. 'Dean Holdsworth can play in an England B international, and then I'll go to Dean and I'll say, "Hey listen, that doesn't matter. You can still come and play for us." Now, I think that's fair until they've played and made their own minds up and actually played in a competitive game. If they play him in a competitive game, that means the country is serious about him being an international player.'

Charlton clearly relishes the new opportunities opened up by the relaxation of the FIFA laws on eligibility which he plans to fully exploit, since England haven't a competitive game till the European Championships begin there in 1996. 'England can't do fuck all about it,' he says, 'because England aren't in a competitive game for the next two years. The only people they can qualify are the kids, the Under-21s who play in competition games. We can make them permanent Irishmen, but the English can't make them permanent Englishmen.'

Charlton offers no apology for the Republic's predatory approach towards the players of his native country. If anything, he says, England have been behaving unreasonably. He accuses them of going out of their way to stop players – among them Trevor Sinclair of QPR and Stephen Froggatt of Aston Villa – from going over to the Irish side.

'I've complained to them,' he says. 'They've qualified a lot of young players who've got genuine Irish parents and who could have played for Ireland. They've given them a cap just to stop them playing for us, and I think that's diabolical. It's not fair and it's not doing the boys any good at all. And I told the pair of them. We could have qualified a lot more players than we have. But we have never qualified anybody we didn't think was going to be good enough to qualify for the national side in the senior squad. We've never been prepared to qualify people for the sake of qualifying them, the way that England have done.'

Taylor, as manager of Aston Villa, signed Froggatt as a youth trainee. When he left Villa to become England manager, Taylor approached Froggatt to play for the Under-21 international side while Froggatt was being courted by the Irish management team and his team-mates at Villa.

'He was not only being chased by Maurice Setters and Jack, but by Paul McGrath, Steve Staunton and Andy Townsend,' Taylor says. 'And I was very much aware of the pressure that he was being put under, which I felt was intolerable coming from senior players. The boy was only 19 or 20 years of age and he couldn't get away from it.'

Taylor dismisses Charlton's allegation about capping players for the wrong reasons: 'I consider that a great insult,' he says. 'We fought for Froggatt. But I would totally deny that Stephen Froggatt or any other player was chosen to play for the Under-21s to stop him playing for Ireland. Stephen Froggatt was chosen because he was good enough.'

'I think Jack gets a bit touchy about this business about the Anglos. I can't see why he should if he doesn't think he's doing anything wrong. As far as I'm concerned he should just go and do it. I have no argument with him because the rules are there and he is using them. John Barnes was born in Jamaica and I had no problem in selecting him.'

Charlton and Taylor agree that the competition for players is growing fiercer, not just with the Republic of Ireland, but between the home nations themselves. Much to the annoyance of the emerging soccer nations in Africa and Asia, Scotland, England, Wales and Northern Ireland are each allowed to field their own international sides even though they come under the one sovereign state. This anomaly means that, in principle, any player holding a British passport could play for any one of the four home nations – Wales could have a team comprised entirely of Englishmen or eleven Scots could turn out for Northern Ireland – but there has long been in place a gentleman's agreement to prevent such a scenario. Under this internal agreement, a player can play for the country of his birth or, where it's different, the country of birth of one of his parents. At the beginning of 1993, the home countries agreed to extend their ruling to grandparents. Thus, for example, a player born in England but with a Scottish grandparent, can play for Scotland. Welcome, England, Scotland, Wales and Northern Ireland, to the granny rule. It has yet to be implemented on any significant scale, though Jonathan Gould, the Coventry City goalkeeper and son of the club's manager, Bobby Gould, has been selected in an Under-21 squad for Scotland, the country of birth of one of his grandparents. The English FA in particular is now faced with losing more English-born players, not just to the Republic of Ireland, but to the three other home nations.

Graham Taylor believes that the FA must do more to meet this challenge, particularly at youth level. 'What the FA needs to provide to the football side of things is a list containing every player who's available to play for England and every player who's got dual nationality. That was never available to me at all unless I went searching for it. The Republic have been far more pro-active at youth level in searching out those players. At the FA there's always been an assumption that if you're English, you'll want to play for England. But there's only so many people who can play for England. What's happening now with the home countries going to the second generation, the pool of players available to play for England is going to be not much more, if more, than any of the other home countries. What you've got to do is get the selection of your players right at the first level, because if you play them in competitive games at youth level that means they're only eligible to play for that country.

'I think the FA are aware of it but I don't think anyone's doing anything about it. There's an attitude that you can't be seen to be scrapping with smaller countries. And what happens is that if you do scrap back, people start to moan.'

The four home nations were prompted to extend their agreement to the second generation by the Republic of Ireland's willingness to make the maximum use of the eligibility laws. Northern Ireland, despite the protestations of Billy Bingham about mercenaries, were particularly keen to increase their selection of players, having been incensed by the loss of Alan Kernaghan to the Republic. 'He's of northern stock,' the IFA secretary, David Bowen, says. 'He had no connection whatsoever with the Republic.'

Anyone born in Northern Ireland can get an Irish passport as well as a British one, if they so choose. It's a logical extension of the Republic of Ireland's territorial claim over the whole island of Ireland. A picture on an album sleeve of the Derry pop group, The Undertones, shows the members of the band holding up their passports as they go on tour – half of the passports are Irish ones, half British. Kernaghan was able to play for the Republic under a complicated law in the Republic regarding citizenship. It means that anyone who has a grandparent born in Northern Ireland before the country of Ireland was divided politically in 1921 is entitled to an Irish passport.

Having greatly increased its pool of players because of its deal with the British Associations, the IFA has tried to stop the FAI from poaching them. Around the time of the World Cup games in Lansdowne Road between Northern Ireland and the Republic, FAI and IFA officials held a meeting in Dublin. The IFA officials sought an assurance from the FAI not to use players with Northern Irish roots who qualified for selection for Northern Ireland, but also had dual qualification for selection by the FAI. The FAI rejected the IFA's proposal, saying that in any such situation it was the prerogative of the players to select the country of their choice.

'Obviously at the moment there is a big incentive for players to choose to play for the Republic,' David Bowen says. 'We felt it was a situation that the two Associations could sort out for themselves, but the officials in the Republic didn't agree. It was a very cordial meeting.'

The IFA's worst fears were realised when it tried to recruit the Bolton Wanderers midfielder, Jason McAteer. McAteer, who had a grandfather from Co Down in Northern Ireland, had come to the attention of the former Northern Ireland international, Bryan Hamilton. Hamilton had been working as a sports journalist for a local radio station on Merseyside and had interviewed McAteer on a number of occasions. When Hamilton was appointed to succeed Billy Bingham as Northern Ireland manager, he immediately stated that he did not share the same objection as his predecessor and let it be known that he regarded McAteer as a legitimate target. The story then appeared on Teletext that Northern Ireland were chasing Jason McAteer. Having opened the door, Hamilton was trampled over by two more powerful suitors.

★

Jimmy Armfield knew that he was up against a formidable opponent when he went over to Bolton on behalf of the FA to offer Jason McAteer the chance to play for England. Himself, Maurice Setters and Jack Charlton went back a long way. Armfield had been in the same army regiment as Setters when they did their national service together in the mid-fifties. Even then, Setters had to do the spade work, cleaning out the stables at Chelsea Barracks, while Charlton's stint includes a period coaching the British army team out in Hong Kong.

Charlton and Armfield had spent much of their footballing lives together. As a full back, Armfield had spent the latter part of his England career playing alongside the obstreperous centre half from Leeds United. At Lilleshall, they had argued vehemently about who should go after the ball when it was kicked over the full back's head. Charlton had argued that Armfield should run back rather than he run over, and had won the argument in the end.

Charlton had views on a lot of things, which is why the *Daily Express* employed him as a columnist, with Armfield, now a trained journalist, as the ghost writer. Armfield had been writing up Charlton's column for ten years before he got the job with the FA. Even when Charlton was out of work, and seen as yesterday's man, Armfield persuaded the *Daily Express* to keep paying him when they wouldn't be getting a column. The most difficult part of it was always tracking Charlton down on the telephone as he was on the move incessantly.

When Charlton's name was linked with the Irish job, Armfield became his *de facto* publicist, briefing Irish journalists and FAI officials about the type of man they were considering taking on board. It was Armfield who phoned Jack at his hunting lodge in the Yorkshire Dales to let him know he had got the Irish job. And then Armfield gave the number to the FAI so that they could get in contact with him.

Now Armfield, in his new role as technical consultant to the FA, was doing a job for the new England manager, Terry Venables. Armfield had spotted a couple of promising boys at Bolton, the right-sided midfielder, Jason McAteer, and the centre half, Alan Stubbs. On Armfield's recommendation, Venables went to see them at Highbury in the fourth round of the FA Cup, when Bolton beat Arsenal 3-1. He decided to pick the two players for a forthcoming England B international against Northern Ireland, and dispatched Armfield to Bolton to inform them of the call-up.

Armfield rang the Bolton manager, Bruce Rioch, to make the arrangements. He was then informed that Jack Charlton was also trying to recruit McAteer and was planning to come to the FA Cup quarter final game against Oldham on Saturday. Armfield arranged with Rioch to see the two lads on the day before the game; it was an arrangement that Rioch was happy with, as he felt it would give McAteer and Stubbs a boost before the big Cup game the following day. Armfield then drove down to Bolton; Burnden Park was familiar territory to him; he had been manager there in the mid-seventies before taking over at Leeds. He sat in the manager's office and called the two players in separately. Armfield told McAteer that Terry Venables had sent him over to ask if he would play on the England B team in a fixture they were trying to arrange against Northern Ireland. McAteer replied that he would be happy to play. He particularly looked forward to playing with Stubbs, who was his best friend.

'He left knowing that I'd be playing for England,' McAteer says, 'and the next thing he sees is that I'm playing for Ireland.'

In the dressing-room after the Oldham game, McAteer shed a few tears. It was the end of a long Cup run, a 1-0 defeat because of a soft goal in the last five minutes of the match. Waiting for him outside was Jack Charlton.

'I said to Jason what I said to all of them. "No pressure. We want you to play for us, but we're not looking to force ya, and if you want to come in and look and you like it, and you decide you want to qualify for us, we'd be delighted to have you." If they qualify for two or three countries, we do that with 'em. And we say, "Listen, there's no hassle. If you decide you want to go play for England, that's your business. But we think you'll like the Irish. Plus the fact that there is an international career with the Irish that might not be there for you with the English. We have only 30 players to pick from, England have three thousand players to pick from."'

Charlton offered McAteer a place in the team for a forthcoming friendly game against Russia, part of Ireland's build up for the World Cup, but he wasn't looking for an answer on the spot. He told McAteer to think about it for a few days and then get back to him.

It was a difficult choice for McAteer to make. 'I'm English, and it would have to be England, I suppose,' he told the Bolton *Evening News* at the time. 'I'm still young and there will be other World Cups. But Jack has dangled an enormous carrot in front of my nose.'

For guidance, McAteer turned to his parents and to Bruce Rioch. His mother, Thora, whose parents were Welsh, wanted him to play for Wales. Rioch had been in a similar dilemma to McAteer; he was also born in England, but played for Scotland, the country of his father. Rioch told McAteer that he would have to make up his own mind, but said he would find it easier to get established with Ireland in the long term.

McAteer dismissed Wales and Northern Ireland. 'The two biggest ones as I would see it are the Republic and England. That's when you start worrying. If it's just one like England, then there's no problems. And when Jack asked me, flippin' heck, it was one of the toughest decisions I had to make since me options in school.

'With England it was like a B international and there have been hundreds of good players who've played B internationals and not gone any further, and it was just, you know, Ireland was a full cap, and I think I can get into the Irish side much quicker than I can with England in my position, because with England it's all blocked off with the likes of Gascoigne, Platt and Batty in there. They're all there or thereabouts, like. I've found that there's no back of the queue with Ireland, it's whoever's playing well that gets in.'

Armfield was left shaking his head. 'I can't understand an Englishman wanting to play for Ireland,' he said. 'No matter how hard I try, I can't understand it.'

The only reservation that Charlton has with the notion of an Englishman in a green jersey comes with the captaincy. In the qualifying round for Italia '90, Charlton had appointed Mick McCarthy as captain. It seemed a logical extension of how Charlton saw McCarthy's role within the side. With qualification assured, Charlton briefly turned his thoughts to matters of etiquette and whom he wanted to lead the side out on to the field. He decided to switch the captaincy from McCarthy to the Liverpool midfielder, Ronnie Whelan. McCarthy was incensed and confronted Charlton. 'I don't know if Jack had been prompted, but he decided that an Irish player should be captain. Ronnie was born in Ireland, played for a high-profile club, the full bit. I disagreed with him strongly over that. I was given the captain's job, it was what I wanted to do, I didn't think it should be taken off me.'

Despite being harangued by McCarthy, Charlton stuck to his guns. 'I always wanted an Irish lad in the early days to be the captain. The captaincy job on the field is not a lot, because everything's programmed before you go on the field. The captain has virtually no decisions to make in a football match. You make them from the touchline, you pass the information on. The captain tosses a coin, he leads by example. Now Mick did that for me wonderfully. But he wasn't Irish-born. And I always wanted an Irish-born captain. Because the jobs to do in Ireland – the visiting the hospitals, the school visits, the meeting of the dignitaries, the introduction of the lads – were better done by an Irishman than an English . . . than somebody born in England.'

Whelan was captain for a couple of games, and then got injured, and the job went back to McCarthy. When McCarthy retired, Charlton was again in a minor dilemma. After Paul McGrath refused the captaincy job, he offered it to Andy Townsend, a Londoner and third-generation Irishman, who had impressed Charlton with his enthusiasm and his willingness to adapt to Charlton's style of play when he replaced Liam Brady. 'Andy is a good lad,' Charlton says. 'He's one of the few people who turns up come hail, rain or high water. He wants to fuckin' play.' He is not however the ideal choice for Charlton. 'If Andy meets Albert Reynolds, he's going to introduce Albert Reynolds to the players in a fuckin' Cockney accent, through no fault of Andy's.'

As the Ireland team arrived back in Dublin from Italia '90, Dublin's pubs were packed with fans desperate for Cameroon to hold onto their lead against England. When a League of Ireland selection team ran out in front of around 30,000 supporters at Lansdowne Road in 1993, there was polite, if somewhat disjointed, handclapping. For their opponents, Liverpool, the reception was euphoric, as the crowd celebrated the visit of their footballing heroes to

Dublin. The irony of the situation wasn't lost on the Bohemians centre half, Robbie Best, who was playing for the League of Ireland that day. 'As a country,' he says, 'we have a very confused attitude towards England. One minute we hate them, next week we love them. Their papers are trash, next thing we buy all their papers to read about the football. It's weird and nobody can really explain it.'

Robbie Best is, as his selection would indicate, one of the best players in his position playing in the National League in Ireland. He is also Robert Best, the pharmacist working in a chemists in Clontarf in North Dublin. His name has been linked with a number of English clubs, Tottenham Hotspur most strongly. Best was well aware that most young Irish footballers – about 95 per cent – don't make it in England, and he had a lot to lose by attempting such a move. At the age of 24, he turned his back on a move across the Irish Sea and then signalled that he was moving outside the pale of the young, enthusiastic and ambitious footballer by launching an attack on the composition of the Irish international side. In an article two years ago in a Bohemians club programme entitled *How Irish is the Irish Soccer Team?* Best stated: 'All in all, I think we are the only nation that has such a collective inferiority complex that we are prepared to have anyone as an "Honorary Irishman" as long as they can guarantee a bit of glory. Jack Charlton has given that bit of glory. In the process of providing it, however, he has compromised us all. He has placed a team of mercenary footballers on a football pitch in green jerseys and given them a structured plan which circumvents their game.

'Let it be made quite clear that Andy Townsend *et al* would preferably have played their international football for England, but they took the well-worth-the-risk gamble of playing for the Republic of Ireland. That this financial gamble succeeded with a green jersey as opposed to a white one is irrelevant to those concerned; they remain professional footballers, not professional patriots, despite the popular myths we, the supporters, like to foster.'

As one of the outstanding players in the domestic League, Best would have been on the fringes of the Irish international side of old. Now, because of the competition, there is no place in the squad for Best or any other National League player – the last one to play for Ireland was Pat Byrne of Shamrock Rovers against Czechoslovakia in 1986. Best accepts the logic of this in purely footballing terms, but in the broader context he feels that too many compromises have been made along the road to success, and he believes the situation has deteriorated further since he made his views known in the club programme. 'Now it's nearly got to the stage where they have an advertisement in the papers saying that if you think you're Irish, please come along and see us. It kind of cheapens everything and compromises the whole thing. I wonder about the people who shout and cheer – maybe they're just making jolly. It's got to be a symptom of the society rather than a symptom of the people. Where we have any bit of success it's grasped so tight that it reflects badly on your aspirations as a nation.'

Vinny Jones came to Dublin in search of a record of his Irish grandmother and instead exposed a raw nerve in the Irish soccer fraternity. Armed with a cunning for self-publicity, Jones had brought a camera crew and a host of journalists with him for a trawl through the Registrar's office for a record of a grandmother whom he was adamant was Irish. 'Begorrah!' ran a headline in the *Daily Star* bestowing Jones with a perceived Irish accent, 'I'm off to pick up my passport now, Jack.'

The British-born players who have declared for Ireland have on the whole been quiet, modest and self-effacing characters happy to do their talking on the pitch. Jones was the worst kind of gatecrasher to the party. In England, Jones was regarded as a hooligan who had crashed down from the terraces on to the pitch gnashing his teeth, licensed by his managers to intimidate star opposition with his manic behaviour. To Irish fans he was the personification of English yobbery, the breed which thousands of Irish supporters had made a point of distancing themselves from in their travels around the world.

Martin Breheny wrote in the *Irish Press*: 'Apart altogether from the ethics of the situation, there is the question of whether the Irish people want to be represented in the international arena by players like Vinny Jones. His disciplinary record and his general attitude on the pitch hardly equate with the standards one expects from international players. Bad enough to have a reputation for shamelessly exploiting the eligibility rules but worse still if the wrong type of player is squeezed in by the back door.'

Jack's initial reaction to Vinny O'Jones, as the English papers were now calling him, was soothing for Irish fans. He told a group of them at a reception, 'We need Vinny Jones like we need a hole in the head.' Then he changed his mind: 'My centre backs are growing old together and I can't see much coming through to fill the gap – Jones might be able to help.'

Jones wore the green jersey when Ireland took the field in the World Cup match against Italy in the Giants Stadium in New Jersey. But he was in Cork, having his stag party with about 50 mates who had flown over from England. He has yet to nail down the birthplace of his grandmother, though he is still trying.

Chapter Thirteen

IT'S A DIASPORA THING

VINNY'S CRUSADE is a lone one, undertaken without the assistance of the FAI. So, should he get all his documents in order, the woman he would be well advised to humour is Marie Byrne at the consular section of the Department of Foreign Affairs in Dublin. Marie is being driven demented at the moment by all those looking for an Irish passport.

Every time there's some more violence in South Africa she and her colleagues groan at the thought of a fresh round of white, middle-class potential refugees ringing through with their queries about how to get Irish citizenship. The chicken run, they call it over there in South Africa. And they're quite brazen about it – some of them will even try to order you about. They'll tell you to your face that they've no interest in living in, or even visiting Ireland. They just want the passport because it's the easiest one to get and it means they can live and work anywhere in the European Community.

The only thing they're interested in concerning Ireland is, will I be conscripted if Ireland goes to war? Mercenaries? . . . Nor does it seem to bother the South Africans that their forebears were mostly of the Unionist persuasion who would roll in their graves if they realised their names were being used to snuggle up to the Fenians. The Americans are the other regular callers. Before they used to get the Irish passport for nostalgic reasons, but now it's mostly business. When the *San Francisco Chronicle* ran an article pointing out how increasing numbers of business people were getting Irish passports while being able to keep their sacred American ones, Irish consular officials in the city were bombarded with queries and applications.

The most unlikely collection of men and women are becoming Irish citizens in sharply increasing numbers. The Irish Foreign Births Register was set up in 1956 and by 1986 there were only 13,000 on the list. Since 1986 a further 30,000 names have been added.

The footballers are only a very small part of it, and they're no trouble either. Jack Kelly from the FAI walks the 200 yards from Merrion Square to Stephen's Green every couple of months with all the papers, which are always perfectly in order. He's a former civil servant so he knows the ropes. Everything is done by the book, of course, but it's a much quicker process than most people think. If everything is rushed through, it only takes about 48 hours.

Marie Byrne can't remember the names of any of the players. Except when Vinny Jones came to town. At first, she thought he was a pop star. Then all the lads in the office started telling her not to give him a passport.

It all started really in the fifties, when the Republic of Ireland, still in its infancy as a sovereign state, turned its attention to its citizenship laws. Thousands of young single Irish women had gone to England, where many had babies outside wedlock. In those days their children couldn't get a British passport because they were illegitimate and there was also no inheritance through the female line. And there's the broader question of emigration itself. As Marie Byrne's colleague, Elizabeth McCullough, says, the citizenship policy is grounded 'in a sense of debt to those Irish who had to leave in the past for economic and political reasons'.

Figures from the Central Statistics Office in Dublin show that in the second half of the 19th century, while the population of most European countries increased considerably, and that of England more than doubled, the population of Ireland was virtually halved, falling from eight million to just over four million. In the ten-year period of particularly heavy emigration commencing with the famine of 1846, the total number of overseas emigrants amounted to some 1.8 million, most of whom were destined for the United States. The next big bout of emigration came with the economic depression in Ireland in the 1950s. Nearly half a million people left the country, a huge loss bearing in mind the smaller size of the total population. Most of these came to Britain, where jobs were freely available in the post-war development of the infrastructure.

The Irish who went to the United States became a strong ethnic grouping, wielding power in the political system, the police and the unions. They became Irish Americans. Irish emigrants in Britain struggled to maintain a strong identity. The institutions which their counterparts in America were able to mould and influence were already in place. They became the nursing and road-building classes, doing the jobs that were unacceptable to most of the natives. The cohesive element to their community was at the social level, at Mass, at GAA clubs or in Irish pubs and dance halls. They lived on the fringes of society. They were the Irish in England. Their children, if they embraced their family background, would be given the derogatory label, Plastic Paddies.

John Lydon was born in London in the fifties. His father was from Tuam, Co Galway, his mother from Cork. On the way to school signs in the windows would taunt him, No Irish,

No Blacks, No Dogs. Lydon later left his mark as Johnny Rotten of the Sex Pistols. But the Irish generally kept a low profile in Britain. Mary Robinson felt the need to light a candle for them at Aras an Uachtarain when she was elected President of Ireland in 1990. They got jobs, some of them got married, had children, and as a group were never heard of again.

But the football team has been responsible for a genuine awakening of popular sentiment – that Ireland belongs to its emigrants as well and its emigrants belong to Ireland.

Peter Carbery, a committee member of the Irish Supporters Club in London, remembers that at a branch meeting several years ago, one member proposed a motion that the parentage rule only apply to second-generation Irish. Another member stood up and pointed out that since he was born in England, such a rule if adopted would mean that his son couldn't play for Ireland. The motion was dropped. 'It was a Dub who put forward the motion,' says Carbery. 'The Dubs are the worst. They're the ones that caused the most hassle when they started going abroad. Mainly because they didn't like the fact that the London Irish had been going abroad since the early seventies. It's only really since the mid-eighties that they have travelled in sufficient numbers. They were saying the usual thing, "You're not Irish. Why aren't you following England?" You fire a quick question at them: "Which football team do you support?" Man United. "What country are they from?"

'There was one classic case; the game against Poland; the three-all draw. We were in Berlin and there's this London-Irish guy, he's as Cockney as anything. He was really winding up all the Dubs. He was saying he was only over here because England were playing in a month's time and they were saying, "Why don't you piss off back to London?" He started asking them questions in fluent Connemara Gaelic and they were looking at him as though he was speaking a foreign language and he says, "You call yourselves Irish. You can't even speak your own language."'

Liam Greenslade from Liverpool took up his job as a researcher at the Institute of Irish Studies in the city at the time of Italia '90. 'As the children of Irish migrants you have very little public validation for your Irishness, unless you are in a major conurbation of Irish people. You find that lots of Irish people grow up with that absence of public validation. The last World Cup team were catalytic in bringing about a public validation for being Irish.

'I never really had a problem with my identity, I always regarded myself as Irish – even though I was born and brought up here. When I came into this job I suddenly found myself being confronted by people who said, "Well, you're not Irish." Both Irish people and English people would say that, and it coincided with the last World Cup. And it was brilliant for me because my immediate response was "I'm as Irish as half those guys you're cheering for, so give me a break on this."'

Dermot Bolger's play *The Tramway End* has an emigrant narrator describing Ireland's match in the European Championship of 1988: 'The crowd joined in, every one of them, from Dublin and Cork, from London and Stockholm. And suddenly I knew this was the only country I still owned, those eleven figures in green shirts, that menagerie of accents pleading with God.'

A science is building up around this football-led phenomenon. Grappling with its terms of reference, Fintan O'Toole wrote in the *Irish Times*: 'Being in the World Cup finals doesn't solve cultural, political or economic problems. But it does make people feel good about their collective self. For good or ill, sport has become a crucial means of self-definition for countries, and soccer, as the greatest international team sport, is the most important of all. In a country like Ireland, which has particular problems in defining itself, the effect is even greater than in countries with more cause for confidence . . . The mongrel nature of the team which has come from Glasgow, London and Manchester, as well as from Irish towns and cities, is the best representation of what it actually means to be Irish now. And for a substantial part of the team's following which is made up of emigrants, major championships offer the possibility of belonging for a few weeks to an Ireland conjured up on foreign soil.'

Jack Charlton's mindset doesn't countenance diasporas. Like Giles, he's a football man, always has been a football man. 'Me bloody mother played football, for Christ sake.' But in football terms, there's a lot of young lads out there with Irish mams and grannies who'd jump at the chance to play for Ireland. A conservative estimate of the number of first, second and third generation Irish people in Britain is three and a half million. Robert Worcester, the chairman of MORI, who has carried out research on the Irish community in Britain for the *Irish Times*, reckons the figure is more like six million. The pioneers – Giles, Hand and Charlton – have only been chipping away at the tip of an iceberg.

Who's to say that by the turn of the century, or before, Ireland won't field a team of eleven players, all of them born in Britain? 'That wouldn't be a problem,' says Louis Kilcoyne, the incoming President of the FAI, 'we'd consider them all Irishmen.' As Jimmy Armfield observed, somewhat sniffily, 'the English League is becoming a training ground for other people's World Cup squads'. That is realism, but allow yourself for the moment a flight of fancy. If soccer catches on in the United States – granted, it is a big if – a whole new horizon opens up. Forty million people there claim Irish descent and Charlton looks great in his baseball cap. The FAI's advertisement for a future manager of Ireland, or perhaps the one after that, might read: 'The Football Association of Ireland is seeking the services of a manager/coach for their national team. Must speak English, preferably based in the United States.'

There are a few potential threats – the possibility of a severe tightening of the Irish passport laws if the European Union decides on a common policy in this area, an awakening by the somnolent English FA to the need for a more aggressive defence of its stock of players, and a change in managerial policy or style by the Irish on the recruitment of players. On the other hand a systematic approach to tapping the resources of this diaspora can yield greater successes. Ireland is no longer a small footballing nation – its supporters can realistically widen the scope of their expectations, Big Jack or no Big Jack.

Few could be as brazen as the big Geordie in the flat cap standing outside the dressing-room saying, 'Do you want to join the Irish?' But if Ireland wants continued, and even greater, success, what it must do, as Charlton would say, is go out there and compete.

Index

190